BEYOND FORGETTING

Many of the poets who contributed their work to this anthology chose to donate their honorarium money to the Al Purdy A-Frame Project to support preservation of the Purdy house in Ameliasburgh and the writer-in-residence programme at the A-frame. Harbour Publishing matched all donations.

To find out how you can support the Al Purdy A-Frame Project and help preserve a living piece of Canada's cultural heritage, please visit their website at www.alpurdy.ca and click on "Donations."

BEYOND FORGETTING

Celebrating 100 Years of Al Purdy

Edited by **HOWARD WHITE** *&* **EMMA SKAGEN**,
with a foreword by **STEVEN HEIGHTON**

HARBOUR PUBLISHING

Harbour Publishing Co. Ltd.
P.O. Box 219, Madeira Park, BC, VON 2H0
www.harbourpublishing.com

Text design by Carleton Wilson
Cover design by Carleton Wilson and Anna Comfort O'Keeffe
Title page photo by John Reeves

Printed in Canada on FSC-certified and 100% post-consumer fibre

Canada Council   Conseil des arts
for the Arts   du Canada

BRITISH COLUMBIA
ARTS COUNCIL
An agency of the Province of British Columbia

Harbour Publishing Co. Ltd. acknowledges the support of the Canada Council for the Arts, which last year invested $153 million to bring the arts to Canadians throughout the country. We also gratefully acknowledge financial support from the Government of Canada and from the Province of British Columbia through the BC Arts Council and the Book Publishing Tax Credit.

Library and Archives Canada Cataloguing in Publication

Beyond forgetting : celebrating 100 years of Al Purdy / edited by Howard White and Emma Skagen.

Poems.
Issued in print and electronic formats.
ISBN 978-1-55017-846-3 (softcover).--ISBN 978-1-55017-847-0 (HTML)

1. Purdy, Al, 1918-2000--Poetry. I. White, Howard, 1945-, editor II. Skagen, Emma, 1991-, editor III. Title: Celebrating 100 years of Al Purdy.

PS8279.B495 2018   C811'.6080351   C2018-904061-0
                                             C2018-904062-9

TELL THE ONES YOU LOVE

Tell the ones you love, you
love them;
tell them now.
For the day is coming, and also the night will come,
when you will neither say it, nor hear it, nor care.
Tell the ones you love.
I have lost many who mattered, and I will say it again:
tell the ones you love, you love them.
Tell them today.

Dennis Lee

CONTENTS

INSPIRATION

LEGACY

ELEGIES

FOREWORD

Steven Heighton

ON TRYING TO WEAR AL'S SHIRTS

The following is an abridged version of a paper delivered in 2006 at the University of Ottawa symposium "Al Purdy: The Ivory Thought."

One afternoon sometime in 1983 or '84, Dr. Leslie Monkman of the Queen's University English Department managed to bring both Al Purdy and Earle Birney into our Canadian Literature class for a reading. I was in my early twenties, just beginning to write poetry, and in awe of both poets. Birney, tall and cadaverous, read first, in a croaky voice, ancient and wavering. He read for about twenty minutes and clearly it taxed him. He had a heavy cold. He seemed to grow smaller and more concave as the reading progressed. He left immediately afterward on the arm of a beautiful young woman who looked as though she could have been a student in our class.

When Al Purdy got up for his turn and peered down at us, the crown of his head almost grazed the bank of fluorescent tubes on the ceiling, or so it seemed to us. In a big, barging voice he prefaced his reading by asking what we had thought of Birney's performance. Nobody spoke. Purdy's high, sunned forehead was stamped with a scowl and his shaded glasses made it hard to decode his expression or even to know exactly where he was looking. After some moments of laden silence I put up my hand and offered that I'd liked the reading but had hoped Birney would also read from *David,* his famous long poem. Purdy stared at me with an unamused grin. A few long moments more and he said, "Yeah, sure, nice old man like that comes here to read, what else are you going to say?" Then he took the toothpick out of his mouth and launched into a long reading, brilliant and riveting.

If I was surprised that Purdy would crack wise about a fellow poet who'd just left the stage—in fact, an older poet, and one who, I later learned, had influenced and encouraged him—it was because I was naive then, maybe a bit wilfully, about a natural and unavoidable aspect of the literary world: the competition. Every poet wants to loom tall. Fiercely competitive poets like Al Purdy aim to loom tallest.

I met him and Eurithe Purdy a few years later, at the famous A-frame in Ameliasburgh, in the summer of 1988. He seemed if anything to have grown taller. Over the preceding years I'd gotten to know his poetry well, this process having begun with an essay I wrote about his Arctic poems soon after he and Earle Birney gave that reading at Queen's. Now Tom Marshall and David Helwig had brought me and a couple of other young poets out to meet him. We sat in a circle of chairs on the deck in the sloping afternoon sunlight and we drank beer and talked. David and Al talked, mainly. Al had only a vague memory of his reading at Queen's and when I reminded him of what he'd said about Birney, he smiled wryly as if to suggest, "I don't remember saying it, but it sounds about right."

A scene from the early nineties, one of our by-now annual summer visits to Al and Eurithe Purdy in Ameliasburgh. Al has taken me into his windowless, clammy, mildewed writing shed. It's above ground but feels like a root cellar. Still air, muffled sounds. From one of the bookshelves he pulls a slim volume—his first published book, *The Enchanted Echo*, from 1944. "Here, have a look at this poem." An awkward moment. These were Al's first published poems. I'd heard he'd disowned them, more or less, but maybe he'd had a change of heart, or had always retained a private affection for the one poem he was now asking me to read. It was clumsily rhymed doggerel, a sort of Edwardian pastiche. I hadn't known Al long enough to be frank. "Well," I said softly, "I think there are some nice sounds in it, but I guess on the whole I prefer your more recent work." Something like that. Al snorted, grabbed the book away and bellowed, "NOW DON'T BE SO GODDAMN MEALY-MOUTHED—IT'S A PIECE OF GODDAMN SHIT!"

Maybe that was the secret of Al's continual improvement. He wasn't just in competition with others, he vied with himself. Was hard on himself. I believe it was Jakov Lind who said that a good writer is somebody who hates himself and loves the world.

I remember saying to Eurithe Purdy, shortly after Al's death, that I thought he was a man who had always taken death very personally. And she said, "Yes, I think that's true." I will add that I think his life's work in poetry was a way of talking back to death, to time and gravity—the gradual attrition of the flesh. In fact Al *competed* with death—not just with other poets, mentors, and himself. I sense that for him this vying with death was the ultimate competition. And the beautiful fuel of his poems.

Al's best poems have, if anything, grown in stature or, as the saying goes, they *stand up*. Maybe I'm just making a case here for aesthetic emulation, since the competitive urge is dangerous to a poet's growth only when its object is status rather than achievement. It's utterly natural but slowly damaging to yearn for plaudits another poet has enjoyed. On the other hand, it's utterly natural but aesthetically *healthy* to read a good poem and then set out to write one as good, or better. It was the second of those urges, I think, that most drove Al's writing.

In the spring of 2000 I saw him for the last time, dying at home in Sidney, BC. Jay Ruzesky and I drove up from Victoria and sat at his bedside for a couple of hours, talking with him and at times just sitting there as we waited for him to wake from another short nap. At one point he tried to eat a piece of bread we brought him, but he couldn't manage. …No eighty-one-year-old, horizontal for the last time, exhausted and unable to eat, rages at the dying of the light. That, after all, was a young poet's prescription. And Al himself—though he took death so personally—seemed at the end to have made a grudging peace with it…

Watching a mentor leave makes an apprentice suddenly feel (like a child watching a parent die) much older. You sense how promise is no longer enough and it's necessary for the real work to begin. Death as the gift of a call to life. The front-line trench, long occupied by elders, who stood between you and mortality and other apparent failures, has suddenly been vacated.

I received one of Al's trademark polyester shirts as a sort of deathbed gift, and in 2006 I wore it while delivering an earlier version of these reflections. I still sometimes wear the shirt because it's my connection to a mentor who understood that I not only loved his best work but envied it, vied with it, took inspiration from the challenge of trying to stand equally tall. I wear this shirt because it's a reminder of all that can't be kept but must be passed on. And to be part of a tradition. And, to be sure, out of love.

INTRODUCTION

Alfred Wellington Purdy published thirty-three books of poetry during his lifetime and forged a reputation as one of Canada's greatest poets. Two of his books, *The Cariboo Horses* (1965) and *The Collected Poems of Al Purdy* (1986), won the Governor General's Literary Award. Over the course of his career he picked up most other awards open to Canadian poets including a special one devised by the League of Canadian Poets called the Voice of the Land Award, a once-only honour to recognize his personification of the Canadian idiom. Like only a few poets in Canadian history, Purdy transcended the literary quarter and forged a profile among the broader public, adding the Order of Canada and the Order of Ontario to his honours, but unlike other poets who succeeded in connecting with the popular imagination, such as Earle Birney and Irving Layton, Purdy is unique in continuing to be a vital presence well into the twenty-first century. This volume of poetic tributes honouring the hundredth anniversary of Purdy's birth amply indicates that he continues to inspire contemporary poets today.

Also unlike many poets of his generation, Purdy still has a thriving readership: since his death in 2000, sales of his selection *Rooms for Rent in the Outer Planets: Selected Poems 1962–1996* have topped an impressive thirteen thousand copies and the book was featured in the CBC's 2006 Canada Reads competition. A larger-than-life bronze sculpture of Purdy has been erected at Queen's Park in Toronto. Wilfred Laurier University Press has published a new selection of his work and House of Anansi Press has published a new edition of his 1962 breakthrough collection, *Poems for All the Annettes*. Two theatrical works featuring his writing have been produced, along with three short films. A feature-length documentary, *Al Purdy Was Here*, was released to general acclaim in 2015. Popular Canadian musicians Gord Downie and Dave Bidini have cited Purdy in their songs and *The Al Purdy Songbook*, an album of musical tributes by such musicians as Bruce Cockburn, Leonard Cohen and Jann Arden, was released in 2018. That year, readings and events were scheduled across the country to celebrate Purdy's hundredth birthday on December 30.

Born and raised in rural Ontario, Purdy dropped out of school at age seventeen to go out west. After serving in the air force during World War II, he worked various jobs while determinedly writing poetry. His first book, *The Enchanted Echo*, which he later disowned, was self-published in 1944. By the time *The Cariboo Horses* was published in 1965, he was able to write full-time, which he continued to do for more or less the rest of his life. To a very great extent his lengthy and productive career was made possible by the assistance of his wife, Eurithe (Parkhurst) Purdy, a Belleville native he married in 1941, who was a superb business manager.

Known for the outspoken and unruly behaviour memorialized in poems like "How I Think of Al" by Susan McMaster and "Purdy's Crocuses" by Tom Wayman, Purdy's personality looms large in his legend, just as his gangling six-foot-three-inch physical being did in life. And yet in spite of his oversized public persona—or perhaps because of it—Purdy is hard to pin down, hard to faithfully describe, hard to do justice to. For he was not *only* the rough-edged iconoclast he was correctly reputed to be; he was an enigmatic—and yes, *sensitive*—man whose entire life was fuelled by poetry.

Jeanette Lynes' poem "English Assignment" playfully invokes the under-represented complexity of Purdy's character as it manifests in his poetry: yes, as anyone who's read his most popular pieces knows, Purdy is well established in the traditions of "Barroom brawl poems" and "Dude poems," but he also essayed many other styles—including tender lyrics like "Winter at Roblin Lake" and what Lynes classifies as "cosmic / ass-kicking poems" like "Gondwanaland."

Purdy's range of interests and poetic forms is no doubt one key to the breadth and durability of his appeal, given that his poetry has touched—and still touches—such a diverse set of readers.

Perhaps more than anything, Purdy is celebrated for his poetic voice—the Voice of the Land as the League of Poets characterized it—a vernacular style unique to himself yet reflective of a universal, pan-Canadian species of English. Writing in a vernacular style did not begin or end with Purdy, but he developed it as an instrument capable of probing the subtlest perplexities of existence in a way nobody had done before and few have attempted since.

Purdy's accessible but profound poetry has found a way into the hearts of readers across the country. He had an even more salutary effect on writers of poetry, having mentored, or at least opened the way for, many younger poets throughout the years such as Tom Wayman, Maureen McCarthy, Lorna Crozier, Steven Heighton, Linda Rogers and many others. And though many of Purdy's followers knew their role model personally, others experienced a proximate closeness through his poetry as Richard M. Grove evocatively recounts in "A Drive with Al Purdy." Even Canadian legend Bruce Cockburn— who wrote "3 Al Purdys" at director Brian D. Johnson's invitation to write a song for the documentary *Al Purdy Was Here* and its accompanying album, *The Al Purdy Songbook*—later credited his experience of reading Purdy's work with reviving his own writing career.

This book also bears witness to a wholly new way in which Purdy's mentoring carries on: through the work of the Al Purdy A-frame Association. Al and Eurithe's lakeside cottage in Ameliasburgh, Ontario, built in 1957 by the Purdys themselves using scrounged materials, acted as a writers' gathering place for decades. After the house was nearly lost to developers following Purdy's death, a group headed by Jean Baird, Howard White, Alexandra Manthorpe, George Goodwin, Duncan Patterson and others—all encouraged by Eurithe Purdy—came to the rescue, raising funds to purchase the property, restoring the buildings and creating a writers' residency program. Few who complete a stay at the A-frame fail to be moved by their own experience of the sights and sounds that informed Purdy's writing, by the history embodied in every scuffed floor tile and by Purdy's spirit, which hovers palpably over the property. The result is a body of work that might be labelled "Looking at Purdy with New Eyes," seen in the work of Doug Paisley, Sadiqa de Meijer, Kath MacLean, James Arthur, Nicholas Bradley, Ben Ladouceur, Autumn Richardson, Rob Taylor and others.

This anthology was instigated by Eurithe Purdy, who, at ninety-four, had never stopped taking care of Al's business. She approached Howard White, Al's long-time publisher, with a folder of tribute poems she had collected over the years. Many of these were published pieces she had photocopied and kept, but some were given to Al and her as private gifts. Rodney DeCroo was surprised and touched to hear that Eurithe had held on to his typescript poem written over twenty years earlier, a charming account of encountering the Purdys called "Al and Eurithe." With Eurithe's pile in hand, the editors first sought guidance from that protean person of letters and veteran anthologist Tom Wayman, whose own career had received a crucial boost after being included in Purdy's seminal 1971 anthology of emerging Canadian poets, *Storm Warning*. Tom did more than offer sage advice; he got the project off to a flying start by preparing a work plan and roughing in much of the selection. That lineup was altered and added to by other hands, but Tom's overall design remains substantially in place. Without his expert intervention, the editors might never have succeeded in putting together this anthology in time to honour Al's hundredth birthday.

Many of the poems chosen speak directly of the poets' encounters with Purdy, either in the flesh or in print, but many do not. Some, such as Peter Trower's elegiac "The Last Spar-Tree on Elphinstone Mountain," are merely dedicated to Purdy. A considerable number by younger writers were inspired by stints as writers-in-residence at the A-frame. Some, like George Bowering's "At the Cecil Hotel" brazenly parody Purdy while still others, like Rachel Rose's "Iowa City" and Ken Babstock's "Cromwell's Head under the Antechapel," are simply fine poems the authors offered in tribute. The whole is remarkably diverse but characterized by an overall vitality that attests to the strong responses Al Purdy continues to bring forth a century after his birth.

ENCOUNTERS

Earle Birney

IN PURDY'S AMELIASBURG

(*first visit 1965*)

But Al   this round pond man—
                where's Roblin Lake   I mean the real one?
                where's that great omphalos I know
                corpsegrey below apocalyptic skies?
        this cosy girl's-belly-button
        brims with rosewater
        from one of those frilly May sunsets

Don't get me wrong   I'm grateful to be here
        after Toronto
                    still hairy from a long winter
        after Trenton
                    that raped that hustled town
it's good here it's peace the blackbirds
are setting off their own springs in the air
        but the air's too bright
it could be I've come the wrong time
        too soon for those horsecrap-fattened peonies
        you reddened the shores with
        too late for skulldeep snow
        stubborn in the fence zags
man there's only dandelions
barring the way to the privy

But no what's wrong is place as well
it's anybody's church across the lake
        the spire shrank
        and that carpenter who fixed it once
        against the sky is off in Trenton
        banging thumbnails and wallboard
        is you in fact

and you're not here   your mouse is hiding
quote representative of an equally powerful race unquote
that heron   the cosmic crying rays
        where in Roblin are they?

In this Ameliasburg a backyard of stones
is where they trucked off Roblin Mill
        declared historical enough
        for reassembly in Toronto
by god they'll whisk your own shack away
if you don't stop writing
        (and Eurithe too the ferocious wife)
        and the very cowpads before your eyes

Al I think they have
I think Somebody's cleaned up
        after your picknicking glaciers
they've raised the roof on the shack
        ringed it with Summer Homes
        told Ptolemy to leave town
        made your spouse patient and young again
it's the Same People of course
        who took the wolves away
        from Malcolm Lowry's woods
        sent Eliot's London Bridge to Arizona
        smoothed Jeffers' headlands back
        into Californian hills
so though it's fine here of course
        it's not Ameliasburg

But wait
        what's popping up when I sweep the kitchen?
                half an envelope
                with half a poem scribbled
and from behind the battered wood-heater

yet another empty bottle
  smelling absolutely of wild grape

Next morning I drift down a nebulous way
   to the village hardware
   like a madman's tiny museum
   Can-opener yep got one
   got one all right You in a hurry?
   yeah got mislaid some time back
   I'd have to look drop in nex week mebbe

I return under the ancient clouds
  the Lake is hazy endless
what bird is flapping away?
the shack's doorknob turns planetary in my hand—
  Al that's your mouse on the floor bowing!

Milton Acorn

KNOWING I LIVE IN A DARK AGE

Knowing I live in a dark age before history,
I watch my wallet and
am less struck by gunfights in the avenues
than by the newsie with his dirty pink chapped face
calling a shabby poet back for his change.

The crows mobbing the blinking, sun-stupid owl;
wolves eating a hamstrung calf hindend first,
keeping their meat alive and fresh...these
are marks of foresight, beginnings of wit:
but Jesus wearing thorns and sunstroke
beating his life and death into words
to break the rods and blunt the axes of Rome:
this and like things followed.

Know that in this advertising rainbow
I live like a trapeze artist with a headache,
my poems are no aspirins...they show
pale bayonets of grass waving thin on dunes;
the paralytic and his lyric secrets;
my friend Al, union builder and cynic,
hesitating to believe his own delicate poems
lest he believe in something better than himself:
and history, which is yet to begin,
will exceed this, exalt this
as a poem erases and rewrites its poet.

Robert Currie

ONCE IN 1965

In a literature class at the U. of S.
—so stuffy my nostrils are clogged—
our prof announces we'll meet next day
in the Arts Theatre and when we do
the place is full of students from other rooms.
"We're gathered together," he says, "to see and hear
a fine Canadian poet who's crossing the land,
promoting a new book." No one I know
has seen a poet before. We wonder
what he'll say, what he'll do.
The man who saunters up to the mic
looks like a carpenter taking a break
from building his own house
with lumber he logged and hewed himself.
"Please, welcome Mr. Purdy," says the prof,
and the poet begins to read, a steam
locomotive roars across campus,
fresh air floods in, poems about Cariboo horses
and home-made beer, hockey players who marry
ballet and murder, not a trace of stuffiness here.
When the poet is finished, one student wonders
if he'd care to discuss tropes in modern Canadian poetry.
Purdy looks at him until we hear ourselves breathe.
"Sure," he says, "you wanna go for a beer?"

Candace Fertile

SENSITIVE MEN

The students watch
entranced
and they laugh as Gord
insults the beer
but drinks the yellow flowers anyway
and then chastises a rooster who knocks over a beer
but says nothing about the guys the rooster has punched out
while beer and blood blossom on the tavern floor
and Al tells his poem
ending with his lament
about the powerlessness of poems
to buy beer
or anything
but Al is wrong
says one student after a lengthy pause
because his poem
bought a place in my brain.

Bruce Meyer

AL PURDY: VOICE

The day had been made in Hades
the way history is thwarted by time
and there's never enough Canadian beer
to wash the air's passion clean
as a starlit November night.
Through the kitchen window
the lost mill of the Roblins
left its reflection in the lake
and a dying seagull
a relic from an old Coleridge number
flopped on the front lawn
as thirsty as a pilgrim of life
but too exhausted to drink anymore.
Halfway through a leak off your porch
you turned to me and noted
with the efficiency of a scholar in your voice
that you'd tried to write your name with water
but wished it had been one syllable less for penmanship
or you'd had just one beer more for pressure.
And I recalled this is the way the animals
mark the boundaries of their minds
their names carved in the scent they leave
with a glass of everything they have taken in
saying simply this is my place
and I will live in it or die.
There is never enough to fill us
though we pour for others
and our names are written on water
not by it
and the ink lake
close enough to see but just far enough so as not to be touched
caught the image of a passing cloud

that looked for all the world like an old plough
and fed it to the mill as grist.
Here my spreading Protean friend
is a promise I made to you as that dying albatross
hungered for the sky even as it clutched the ground
that wherever I sail
whatever zephyrs press me on
I shall write my name on a wall or passing rock
to declare the truth that I was here
measuring my thoughts in syllables and piss
that a common man might take for history
the way you taught me
when we gave our names to the earth.

David Helwig

AL ON THE ISLAND

Striding off the ferry
in Eurithe's white chapeau
you are taller than anyone.
At seventy-nine and warned
to keep yourself out of the August sun,
frailer flesh and less amused,
sober on doctor's orders
you still grab up
a wide space in the air.

You have to bend your head
at every doorway here,
the house too small, the car
too small, besides
it's running out of gas
and you don't intend to walk.

You've smelled mortality
and the smell annoys you.
When someone says Earle Birney
had no real friends,
well, that annoys you too.

After a sort of lunch
there's not that much to see,
thin soil, sun-stricken fields,
rolls of hay. The small deer
gone somewhere out of sight.
And the gas is getting low.
"I mean it, you better
turn back. The tank's
on empty, and I'm not walking."

There are books to be sold
at a store in Kingston, one way
to turn a dollar except
you always keep too many,
looking for the old secrets
you can put to use.

Between memory and possibility
the poems compose themselves
at night by flashlight
scribbling in the dark.
Might as well keep on,
you've done it all your life,
learned how to say
the words that come between
time and silence,
in a voice that went
beyond itself and came back
with news we've never heard
or almost forgot,
something almost human
(as you might have said)
and almost not.

Russell Thornton

PURDY'S OTTERS

I too visited Al Purdy
when he lived in Sidney, BC.
I acted as the chauffeur
for his old friend
the poet Marya Fiamengo,
whom he invited
to his and Eurithe's home
for a late-in-life tea
after not having seen Marya
for more than a few years.
Creaking as he got up
from the couch, grumbling
a little more each time
Eurithe asked him to go
up the stairs to the kitchen
and put the kettle on,
and carry back down
another fresh pot of tea,
lumbering stooped,
obviously taxed by the job,
he was still unfailing
in getting that tea for us.
I was all ears
while he and Marya
brought up Canadian poets
and exchanged snark
about this one,
praise for that one,
also while they discussed
BC Medical and OHIP benefits,
(which I knew things about
because I took care

of my elderly grandparents—
and I piped up).
Then Al announced
that he and I might as well
go down to his library
in the basement,
where he proceeded
to show me the prize item
in his collection
of Victorian pornography,
replete with writings
and large illustrations
(a few years later, I saw a photo
of him holding up
the same book, and realized
he had probably shown
a lot of people
that particular volume).
He read a passage
out loud with great glee.
That's how it is, isn't it? he said,
a grin on his face.
Yeah, I guess it is, I said.
I figured he was teasing me,
but couldn't be at all sure
(and I could see he liked that).
What I remember most
of the afternoon, though,
was going outside with him
to walk around the property.
I'd been calling him Mr. Purdy—
suddenly he said, softly, *Al.*
And there was a moment
when it seemed he wasn't
peering down at me
from his 6'3" to my 5'8" anymore—

no, instead we were both
around four and a half feet tall
and around nine years old.
See, he said, *otters come up*
this creek from the sea
just down there.
It's the best thing
about this place.
They're quivery, quick
little things, gone in a flash.
They're not here
right now, but they
often are. Come back anytime
for another visit. You'll see.

Katherine L. Gordon

INTERVIEW AT EDEN MILLS

Colourful crowds gathered on a grassy steep
overlooking the ruins of the storied Harris Woollen Mill.
Shelagh Rogers sat across from Al for a last interview,
his manner flinty as the stone
not accommodating the superfluous or ingratiating.
He parried with a humour gleaned
from observation of our fickle species,
his life already detached from the fray
but celebrating it as keenly
as a whiskey at a wake.
My last encounter, fixed in memory's favourite corner,
of a fiercely talented poet seer,
who shaped a nation's vision,
lifted us out of formal connections of habit
to an appreciation of a raw Canadian perspective
with the courage to paint it in vivid free verse,
conferring value on the everyday drama
transforming it to vibrant art of life.
Al's "ordinary" always the undertow of extraordinary.

Brian Brett

from REAL LIFE—CAN YOU IMAGINE IT?

Al Purdy at the window
looks over the farm while
the peacock fans a white goose
and the evening sun flames
on the burnished leaves of the giant maple.
Then he turns to me and says:
"Real life—can you imagine it?"

Douglas Fir,
Arbutus,
Garryana Oak,
     miles and miles of them,
     reaching down to blue ocean
     where illuminated ferry boats
     glow unearthly in a sea mist.

Can you imagine it?
Is it real?
What's real?

You couldn't,
you shouldn't,
you wouldn't.
     You might get shot in Salvador.
     A redback spider could bite your ass.
     The parrot will say good morning.
     An igneous rock hardens near the earth's core.
     The aliens are introduced to Elvis Presley.
Can you imagine that?
     Yes, I think I could.
Elvis Presley always was an alien.

For that matter,
who could imagine
        Al Purdy,
an ageing poet at the window,
and is he real?

Real life—a trick, a joke
a quest to find what shouldn't exist at all—
        the spirit?
The only part of the body which doesn't
survive the atomic swirl of chemical
        action and reaction?

Who could have imagined all of this?
Not God in a vacuum some place near
where the Vega galaxy originated?
It's too hard to imagine
a vacuum with imagination,

and harder still to define
God as an explosion
with such creative flare.

The big bang invented finger painting?
The lord of the unreal universe
designed bad porno pictures?
        Encephalitis?
        30 foot long tapeworms?
What kind of God is that?
What kind of universe is this?
Who could have imagined it?

Linda Rogers

FAMOUS LAST LINES

I knew how to cultivate asparagus.
Just like poems, it likes manure.
Bullshit, the voice of the land said
when he pulled his famous last lines
out of the compost. That wild man
knew he couldn't force words any
more than he could grow a turnip.

He had to find them. Like children
waiting in the forest to be discovered
by the right parents, his poems hid
under cabbage leaves, or dangled
from the beaks of Valkyries looking
to reverse the tolls of war and natural
selection. Verse lurked here and there,
everywhere the poet searched, from
the fenced pastures of Prince Edward
County to the minarets at Samarkand.

Unlike poetry, which isn't particular
whether it grows in sun or shade, in
the sand around ancient monuments
or ice floes cruising the Beaufort Sea,
the wild asparagus called out to him
from Ameliasburgh ditches as precious
as the wisdom written in ancient script.

Then as now, every green stalk an
epiphany, every mouthful a poem.

Doug Paisley

WHILE YOU WERE OUT

Thought I should leave you a note
I was here while you were out
I could tell by the furnishings and the magazines
You'd been gone a long time
I answered the phone, it was for someone else
I even saw your tombstone in the cemetery
I found your leather coat behind a door
Put it on
Sat down on the porch to smoke
I began to creak like an old club chair in your coat
Later in a photograph of you in the yard
I saw a sapling at the fence line
I turned to the window and the trunk reaching out of sight

When it got dark I locked your door and went to bed
What was I afraid of?
I had a dream about a boat in a marsh
That I nearly missed
There was something I had to do
A pump was thumping behind my head
The shoreline was flooded and water was up against the side of your house
How nice it would be not to worry about that anymore
Some friends were stopping by
Before guests arrive I'm always tense
Like a fugitive
Maybe that's what makes gossip dreadful
When you're gone people can only talk about you

Sadiqa de Meijer

ANCESTOR VS. ANCESTOR

The darkness then was darker than we know;
it never left the corners of a room,
rose velvetly from cellars, where it blinded the potatoes—
like curd it formed a film on wooden spoons.

Grains of darkness clustered in the orchards.
Dark moisture kept the cabbage leaves apart.
All over the old country, there were nights. No hands, no ground.
You've never really seen the stars.

And what was in it? Spectres, wraiths—
they spooked the horse. Some things that people did.

A continent was dark. It could be what we wanted.
Animists, ivory, pith of strange fruits.
We must have been, for all intents, asleep.

When those nations flickered and were lit,
there was no fault to speak of.
And we didn't speak of it.

James Arthur

IN AL PURDY'S HOUSE

It is strange, living in the house
of a writer who has died. I use your cutlery,
your typewriter. I read your autobiography
while lying in your bed, trying to imagine Roblin Lake
and this lakeside piece of land
as they were sixty years ago, when you and Eurithe
built the A-frame by hand,
with no experience of carpentry, using salvaged lumber
and whatever materials you could find.

Critics seem to always talk you up or talk you down,
casting you as the forerunner
of all Canadian poets who were to follow,
or else as a roughneck and a clown.
For me, it's enough that you were endlessly demoted
during a war you found unreal;
that you lived and wrote according to an image
you had in mind;
that you called your house *A drum for the north
wind, a kind of knot in time.*

Your mother's good china
is still here, asleep inside the hutch. History,
your personal history, hangs around the record player,
which I haven't dared to touch—
but this year there's been so much rain,
Roblin Lake has climbed up fifteen feet on the grass,
making an island of the short peninsula
you and Eurithe added to the shore.

Standing at the window near the kitchen,
watching a single sailboat pass
back and forth across a distance
that couldn't be more than a mile from end to end,
I feel a collapse of distinctions
between the real and the unreal,
between what has already
taken place, and what is happening right now,
as if time had been doubled over into itself,
like a sheet of folded steel.
Cottage country becomes backcountry,
as houses along the shoreline
blink out and disappear.

I know better than to make myself at home
in a house that isn't mine.
Soon, I'll leave the keys
on the counter, turn the lock
on the inside, step out, and close the door—
and from that point forward
there won't be any of this, anymore.

Maybe because I'm left-handed
I made my way through your collected poems
back to front,
so I ended with the love songs of a young man—
poems for women
you seduced, or thought you might seduce—
and I began
with your regrets, the many places you visited,
and your elegies for friends
who during my backward progress
came to life one by one.

Grace Vermeer

TRANSIENT

I was searching for Al Purdy on Dundas in London,
Attic Books, second floor, poetry section
when the phone rang. It was Al, calling to say
he was riding the boxcars out of Winnipeg,
headed west toward Regina with a drifter.

This guy wants a handout, but there isn't
a sandwich in two hundred miles—just a minute,
he wants a smoke.

I stood there and listened, he rustled around
in his pockets, found a cigarette, then a match.
That's the thing about Al, you can stand there
on the rumbling roadbed while he draws a map,
you think you're holding summer in your mouth,
then you notice—
no arrivals, no departures,
it's just you, standing there, getting old,
and then older.

Rodney DeCroo

AL AND EURITHE

sitting in the vancouver press club
with al purdy and his wife eurithe
feeling uncomfortable
not sure what to say to the man
whose every poem i've read and admired
whose voice sounding the depths in my head
has become more familiar
than those of my friends
right up there with my wife's voice
but there are places in me
his poems have touched
marked keep out even to her
so what do you say to a man
whose words have opened
rooms in your head
you didn't know existed
what do you say

not much
because there are no words for it
except maybe
fireflies sparkling in the brain
or
fox fox fox
which i can't say because
he's already said it
so i shut up
grateful he's more than willing
to direct the conversation
yet i sit there feeling like
a six year old nodding and agreeing
with everything he says forgetting

i ever had a thought of my own
jumping up to get peanuts from the bar
when eurithe says she's hungry
wishing i could stop myself
feeling like polonius must have felt
a stuttering sycophant
fawning and scraping
at the skirts of royalty

but they aren't exactly royalty
more like an old odd couple
trying to make an extra buck
at the local flea market
hawking al's books spread across
the table the prices written out
in black marker on a piece of cardboard
al arguing with eurithe about a pen
he's lost eurithe says never existed
cutting him off saying al it's not worth it
in a tone my grandmother uses to warn my
grandfather the discussion has come to an end
i go to light up a smoke
and al says eurithe is allergic
to cigarette smoke cats and him
eurithe smiling thinly through pressed lips
al's getting impatient
complaining loudly because he wants to read
so he can get back to the sandman inn
to watch the news and get some rest
he stands up a bit shakily
to go corner the organizer who's running
around trying to organize
not doing a very good job of it
leaving me to make small talk with eurithe
who is pleasant enough but she knows this is al's night
that's why i'm here

so when i botch her name introducing her to friends
she says bluntly i'm mrs. purdy
sparing me any further discomfort
for which i'm grateful

al's back
all six foot something of him
peanut shells and spittle
at the corners of his mouth
i want to wipe it off thinking
good god man
you're a literary giant
which he is but that doesn't spare you
the traits of other mere mortals

the reading starts
three local poets on stage
ten minutes into their reading
al lurches up nearly knocking
over the table shouting
how goddamn long do i have to wait
then marches out the front door
with the organizer following
tailed by eurithe to negotiate
you can hear al
bellowing outside on granville street
while everyone pretends not to hear
the poets continuing to read
tension filling the room
like when a parent behaves badly
at the dinner table
the kids afraid to say anything

door bangs open as they come back in
al sitting down his arms crossed glaring
as if defying me to say anything

i stare back not wanting to look a coward
when eurithe says jokingly
al think sweet thoughts
or you'll have a bad reading
it's al's turn
he's up there working his magic
the audience is laughing
this curious old man
who's so much himself
he fills the whole room
i'm listening to the poems
getting lost in that twilight space
where time stands still or suddenly speeds up
momentarily glimpsing the hairs of my soul
in the flux of another man's words
my defects forgiven
in that straining to be human
a gift he's given me so many times.
i'll never get his voice out of my head
when i glance over at eurithe and
she's nodded off to sleep

the reading's over
a crowd hovering around the table
congratulating al on being al purdy
while buying his books i excuse
myself to go sit with some friends
saying a quick goodbye promising
to return al's letter at which he smiles
then al and eurithe leave slip out early
al counting in his head
the take for the night
eurithe just wanting to get some sleep
exhaustion all over her face
suddenly i'm ashamed of putting al up
on the mantelpiece of my icons

making him less than human
wondering if i've ever really read his poems
i want to run out to the street
shout wait have a good trip
hoping al sold enough books
and eurithe will have a good sleep
before the long trip back to the island—

so thanks al
for the poems
for being so much yourself
you had to write it all down
helping us to see ourselves
inhabiting eternity and the shining mountains
in this too brief allotment of time
where only the saying of things is possible
and goddamn it
you said it well

June 1996

David Zieroth

I MET YOU ONLY ONCE, AL PURDY

… but that was enough to know
your bluster wasn't all of you
and if we meet again in the west
where souls are said to go
which you didn't believe in
and which sometimes I do though
not today, one day closer to my own
departure, would I be nervous around
a giant like you, whether I mean
teetering from wild grape wine
or heads taller than us who followed?

but supposing we do meet there
let it be away from crowds, those
worshipping, those stabbing, let's stay
outside where we're invigorated
by a touch of northern air
coming down from that arctic
above our heads, the scent
of rhododendrons reminding us
distance is time more than space
and I'll be wanting you to talk because
your voice says more than words

and it hardly matters there
what is said, companionship's
the point, not warmth exactly since blood
has left us, our cravings and unfinished
lives of no interest yet aren't we even so
still writing? the way thoughts keep
starting up despite the urge to record them

having ceased, and no pen
or portable Underwood

our physicality spent, and only angels
—or demons—to brave, but surely
we'd be free, neither of them wanting
our insubstantiality now our mouths
are full of dirt back where we left them
once upon a time
ardently believing what they said

Howard White

A WORD FROM AL

Being dead isn't so bad, in fact it has a lot going for it
Not so different from being alive in Ameliasburg
Which was my favourite thing to be before this
It was time for a break from eternally trying to top my own best lines
Except that wasn't eternal as it turns out, a mere spark of time I see now
I guess I always knew it was a small window I had to make my mark
To leave some words that might hold a place in the living world
Something I thought important for reasons I can't quite recall now
It made me impatient with bullshitters and small talkers
Forever stepping around the elephant in the room
Me forever saying "what is this fucking mammoth doing here?"
I was born impatient to break skin, draw blood, get to the heart of the matter
And I got a lot of flak for that, was shunned for lack of social grace
I could see how it made the better-bred avoid me and feel hurt
Like that time in the Cecil I razzed Curt Lang about fucking his mother
Or at least really wanting to, when they squatted in the old Vancouver Hotel
He blubbered and stammered denials in front of those wide-eyed strangers
He'd been trying to impress with his *Übermensch* act
I could never resist a target like that and anyway it did him good
To face whatever demons drove him from poetry to profiteering
Not keeping at any one thing long enough to make any real mark
Which is not something anybody could say about me
Despite a knockabout life in which no other one thing was constant
Except maybe poverty and my on-again/off-again contest of wills
With that amazing woman, the most amazing thing about her being
The way she hung in with me through all those years of trial and betrayal
And even says some half-assedly good things about me now that I'm safely gone
People, men that is, thought she was a hard case and asked what held me
Or at least kept me coming back after my many inconstancies
But it was just that hardness, as hard as reality, as real as poetry
That grounded me and gave me a north star to plot my rambling by
And not to be overlooked is the fact she always took me back.

Was that love? It is not a word we had much use for, but whatever it was
It was more enduring, more forgiving, more sustaining than any other
Rotten husband as I was, nobody can fault my faithfulness to my true mistress
Not Eurithe but Euterpe, the muse I served with far greater devotion
From the time that old fraud in a cape declaimed before my high school class
To those last scribblings I left on top of the fridge before I took the hemlock
I lived for nothing else but the magic word that would uncork the lightning
For the place and mood that would allow me to be the instrument
Of the good and true poetic utterance that would be seen as good and true
And despite everything including a complete lack of qualification
I did stay true to that purpose and I did write some poems
That must have been good, despite what the world's bartenders thought.
They are easier to abide than those self-appointed champions I must endure
As I lie here beside this stagnant millpond weighted down
By the half-ton book of stone Eurithe placed to hold me till she comes
Droning on about inconsequentials like my drinking and fighting
The bullshit persona people constructed around me that was never me
Or was never more than the skin I wore like an old shirt from the Sally Ann
While I went about my business of courting that most fickle of muses
Like a blind man obsessed with capturing butterflies
And not just any butterflies, but the rarest and most breathtaking
And sometimes, against all odds, succeeding.

Richard M. Grove

A DRIVE WITH AL PURDY

Al Purdy drove with me
up the 400 highway to Barrie
the 2 AM waste land
north all the way to our cabins
up and down indigo hills
chasing shafts of light
wincing with the click, click
of bugs on windshield.

He regaled me with his genius
poem after poem never stopping.
He started with "At the Quinte Hotel"
he and I, sensitive men, driving
out of chaos into quiet,
through the ghosts of his past
blurred by speed
heading into my present.

We drove through draping mist
that clung to Al's every word,
pungent, penetrating, succinct
and then the tape came to an end,
I drove the rest of the way
in silence. His words still hanging
from branches of tall trees, sparkling
through cloudless sky over
red polished Cambrian shield.

Uncle Al's words whispered to me
unspoken as I walked down
our shrouded black lane
onto dew-covered deck.

WILDNESS

Milton Acorn

PROBLEM

When you look into your golden beer
and talk about suicide, Al,
I can't help dreaming laments,
obituaries, and how craftily
I'd cull my quotations
of you; half martyr
to this dusty tasting time
and half damned decadent.

Like a green lignum vitae tree,
a nuisance on the lawn,
dead you'd carve into strong shapes,
living you're a problem.

Milton Acorn

POEM FOR AL PURDY

With crowbar looks, tossing rock words,
let's bash each other's cages.
You're caged man...I can see the bars.

Switch your tail like northern lights
with stars glinting thru it.
Pace...Pace.
How bone swings muscle and muscle bounces bone!

I twist among coiled currents of breeze
rolling in the sun
and leaves drinking light, air,
atom by atom.

But there's something I only touch
thru a pillow of wind.
Something out there...I want it.

Don't just make another me,
a doll for your cage.
Bash...Bash.
You're caged man...I see the bars.

My own, I can't see.

Julie McNeill

ACORN AND AL BUILD SOMETHING

Pass me
> *your pencil*
> *your glasses*
>> *Did you measure this?*
How about a light?
Let's take this to the window.
See what scribble amounts to in this place

You call this
> *a line?*
> *a verse?*
> *a cabin?*

Pass me a cigar.

Rolf Harvey

"YOU HAVE TO KEEP WRITING!"

We did some things that were wrong
socially and perhaps that is all—
Porter's house rolling on the floor
with her dogs so we were covered in hair
when Julian came home
to insist we leave by cab.
Anna brushed us off.

Or that time when I was renting
half a house in Rosedale
when my friend came to visit
and blew my trumpet out the window
at 1 a.m. in Rosedale.

So the neighbour's daughter rang the bell
and asked my wife, who was younger
and knew better: "please ask your father
to stop playing his saxophone."

Ruth said it was a trumpet. Closed the door.
We called my friend a cab
but not before a lot of hoo-hah
and his constant reminder
to write all the time.

Hell, people need their sleep.
The world doesn't run on poetry.

And that is why he had to live out there
pissing on his own lawn,
staring up at the sky in wonder.
Always building a bit more onto

that point of land
out into the water
away from his neighbours
so he could howl.

"Just keep writing," he said
as he got into the taxi.
"You have to keep writing every day."

He spoke to himself hoping I would hear.
My friend meant what he cried out
because it was his only way.

Sid Marty

MY EDITOR

in memory, Al Purdy and John Newlove

I phoned him from the Purdys' at 1AM
Al's idea; it seemed
reasonable, at the time.

The first thing John said was
"Stay away from the sink."

He'd broken his ankle weaving round
that homely receptacle.
Something about spilled water, beer
and arguing over poems.
The usual debacle (statistics prove
most accidents do happen in the home).

They'd put in pins; he had much pain, but
from what I know, I think he got off lucky.
Anyway, he claims
the leg's two inches shorter now.
He'd noticed it while crutching in
to be measured for a suit.

"That's why I always stick with jeans,"
I told him.
"Stay clear of doctors, tailors
anyone equipped to measure bones."

I don't know what they had him on, but
"Listen," he said, in that
late night DJ undertone—it always
drew me in, as co-conspirator.

"Something you can do for me.
Little favour. For your editor.

"Listen closely now," he said
with voice that took a rising edge
of menace. "When Al passes out
just cut about two inches
from his right leg
—make sure you get the marrow.
And bring it to Toronto
packed in ice.
Now will you do that for me?
I need it for a transplant.
This goddamn ankle isn't healing right."

"Ha! I don't think Al
would go for that,"
I chuckled.

"I'll be waiting at the station,"
said my editor, breathing hard.

"Okay, John, get serious." It was
the wrong thing
to say. The phone vibrated in my hand
and I could feel him leaning on that wire
like a grim, meat-eating bird.

"Look, chum, you want me on this book
or not? Just say the word."

"Well, shit, the guy's a friend, you know."

"Look, he won't even miss it,"
my editor cajoled.
"He never uses that leg."

I felt the sweat bead
in my thinning hair.
Young poets need an editor
like Jesus needs the devil,
and the devil needs his exorcise;
they're mates, coeval.

I shot a furtive look
at my recumbent host,
lost in a cloud of cheap
cigar smoke, on his divan.

Al looked about as sleepy
as an irritated grizzly
and was no slouch at truculence, forsooth.

"John, I dunno.
I lack tools for major surgery
as well as a medical licence."

"C'mon," he said, "I know you're an EMT.
They have a hacksaw there
that's all you need."

(I can see now I was succumbing
to my editor's spell.)
"It seems so drastic somehow, man,"
I whined. "Why not wait for a donor
to drop dead, like everybody else?"

"Because I need a poet,"
breathed my editor.
"Get the picture?"

It made my blood run cold.

"Until tomorrow, then.
We'll talk about your script.
Just make sure you get that marrow:
bring it
with
you…"

"So how is he?" demanded Al
suspiciously. "Did he sound bitter?"
"No more than usual," I replied

and I cracked another brewski,
dodging Al's appraising eye,
tried to deflect with
"I think he's got some more
healing
left to do."

Then I went outside to drop a litre.
Thought about Al's famous poem
trying to piss upon a star.
But the breeze was up on Roblin Lake,
so I focused on not pissing on a stair.

Banff, Alberta, 1979

Wednesday Hudson

FOR AL

Al
my stack of failures loom like the goddam Rockies
I see every morning
when I drop that big kid off at the fancy school
(that appeases my guilt for failing as his mother)
and the grief catches up to me
like the next small town on a road trip
and I wish you were here
with a glass of Ameliasburg wine
but you're not even alive
and for now, it's my turn

I guess I'll just write
write
to try and right a lot of wrongs
like a marriage that got too broke to fix
the wrenches piled up, along with the towels
and there's nothing for me to stare at—
no lake, no Eurithe
no Milton to curse at—
just me and the walls of an echoless bedroom
freed from the snores
of a hairy man I'm sure to love and hate
'til death do us part—
even though we're no longer together except
at opposite ends of front doors
watching our genes-that-came-together
cross over the gulf of a family in splinters

I haven't built a house for my self yet Al
I know there's a stack of scrap lumber
in those failures of mine

some dirty work to do
some nails to pound
some blisters to spawn

how to architect them into a wholly different tale
that just might end in redemption of shit to flower?

Tom Wayman

PURDY'S CROCUSES

They say when Al Purdy
was poet-in-residence at Loyola
he would drive up to Montreal Tuesdays and Wednesdays
and enter the office they had given him
with a 12-pack of beer under each arm.
For two days each week he would sit
talking to students, looking at poems or whatever, and drink
and toss the empty bottles out the window.

This went on all winter. In the spring
they say the first thing that appeared out of the melting snow
under Purdy's window was a beer bottle
and then another, as one by one
a whole term's pile of empties was uncovered
and they say the students called them
Purdy's crocuses.

Since hearing this, wherever I drive
—west along 17 from Sudbury
across the Wawa wilderness, or east
on 16 through Jasper from Tête Jaune Cache—
I don't mind so much the dozens of empty beer bottles
strewn in ones and twos beside the asphalt, sometimes accompanied
by water-soaked bits of cardboard from their cases
but mostly not. I like to think

what the poet planted in Montreal
has taken hold, spread coast-to-coast
like a new brand of cigar or rabbits in Australia:
slowly the shoulders of the main highways, and the ditches
along every back road in Canada
are filling with the brown blooms of Purdy's crocuses.

Gregory Betts

SHOULDERS DESCENDING

Al Purdy pushed me down the stairs,
his massive hands, the kind you make
oversized statues of, warped their vein-
laden declamation around my once-
broken collar bone, while his fingers
caress the ridge of bone. I touch posters.
Exhale into the open street night below.

I've never seen anything like it, he says,
as we step down from the Imperial Pub,
stutter stepping like mournful elephants
retreating from a burial, bush-whacked
alligator pie-eyed, stoners from Rochdale,
his long arms trailing between us, something
British Columbian, syllables that slur. We kick dirt
over the evening, his second hand
ticking into my neck. I've been in a lot
of bars, you know, even poetry.

I've seen fights, seen people fucking,
I've seen poets read essays they had no
right to read. The freedom to destroy.
We stumble, I grasp the rail
(down to its last spike), as we bump and
plough awkwardly down to Dundas. I am
supporting too much of Canadian literature
on my shoulders. There would be consequences
if I were to slip. Broken bones heal, but
national literatures are much more fragile.

Did you know, he says suddenly, that the
stirrup-shaped bone in your middle ear

is the smallest one in your body? A broken
one's never been found, so small.
We pause for cadence, as if to listen to
its lack of size,
only hear the gentle scratch
of Dennis Lee signing papers
back in the bar. Something indelible.

When we make it to Toronto, his hand
quickly cups my head. He winks, walks off
to Halifax in a gale of snow faded caribou,
a lethal puff of smoke from a diesel thug,
the city unfolds like a rolled-up mattress,
folds back up and ferries off the way words
sometimes hover sometimes disappear altogether.

K.V. Skene

AS THE DAYS AND NIGHTS JOIN HANDS

after "The Dead Poet," Al Purdy

hold onto our self-absorbed selves
brisk as whisky-jack weather   strong
as a vagabond's song   broken
as last year's wedding vows

while our bright little Wi-Fi lights
wink with the superior insight
of fraught battles
and innovative ways of becoming

and we speak hope in its fullness
a language of uncertain syntax
and unsustainable joy

as if in this one inarticulate moment
our every word will become
a light unto the world.

Susan McMaster

HOW I THINK OF AL

—as he walked right into it
in the packed and beery bars,
as he taunted the young poet,
why do it, if you find it so hard,
as he barked his knuckles,
scarred his hands,
pulling nails from old planks
to bang together a home,
as after four months
of cold and dirt and dark
by my own frozen lake
in my own dank cabin,
I heard death yodel,
as he returned time and again
to the one who let him in
when his wanderings ran out,
as I realize on this night
of dead ashes and yellow moon—

Al, you're not my muse.
But some part of you
is stuck in my words
as they rise from the cedars
with mosquito buzz and night hawk,
as they fall into my hands
in the Gatineau hills
cold and soft as snow.
I think of you, Al,
as you go.

George Bowering

AT THE CECIL HOTEL

translation of Al Purdy's "At the Quinte Hotel"

I am writing
I am writing another goddam poem
about drinking beer
and it's clearly obvious that I'm an artist
And I figure that the bartender is an artist as well
so I show him my beer poem draft
mainly the part about the draft
he poured me that tastes a lot
like a Milton Acorn poem
But it seems that the bartender
is more into nonfiction prose
the way he turns his back
and lets out an anapestic fart
Across the semidark room
two women with large arms
and large tattoos on their arms
are drinking ale and writing poems
They pay no attention
to the two bony guys slugging each other
with grimy fists. "Pat Lane
couldn't carry Newlove's jockstrap!"
says one bony guy as he slips
in the beer and blood on the floor
and the other guy kicks him in the ear
After a while the guy picks himself up
and staggers over to his table
and sits down with a beer and a book of poems
Now the beer in my belly
is looking for a way out
but I have to pass the other bony guy
on my way to the dimly lit pisser
I can't help myself

being an artist and all
I told him "Dorothy Livesay could wipe the floor
with Newlove and Lane and Alden Nowlan!"
"Wanna come outside and say that?" he says
so I go outside and say it again
He takes a wild swing and falls down
and I sit on his head
which is face down in the parking lot
"Out here in Vancouver the poets
make love, not war!" I instruct him
He lifts his hand in a peace sign
and I let him up because I'm an artist
When we get back inside
there's a guy with a big bony nose
and a bag full of mimeographed poems
"A dollar a poem," he says
"or I will read you five pages for a beer!"
I ask him what kind of poems they are
and he says "Immutable, inscrutable, marsupial!"
I buy five of them and hand him a beer
because I've heard of this guy
He rides a bicycle all over town
and jams mimeographed poems in mail slots
He has recorded every poetry reading
ever given in this town
"Welcome to the Cecil!" he says to me
"I can tell that you are an artist
writing poems in a beer parlour—
you are contumacious, salubrious, bituminous!"
And he was out the door and off on his bike
before I could show him
my latest occasional poem
with him in it, him and beer and blood
Now I am an artist without a dime
an artist without a beer
and likely to remain that way.

INSPIRATION

F.R. Scott

THIS INN IS FREE

I will arise and go now, and go to Roblin Lake,
To a cottage NORTH OF SUMMER, with PURDY on the door.
I'll arm myself with hard tack, some rat-poison, and steak,
And sleep alone on a hard-wood floor.

When dawn comes through the window, with bird-song à la crow,
I'll rise and light my candle, and search for things I love,
And wrapping round my blanket, to warm me as I go
I'll creep my way to the unlit stove.

When AL comes down to join me, I'll greet him with a grin.
My books will all be ready, my voice will be so sure,
That though he'll try reciting before I can begin
I'll blast him with my OVERTURE.

Then will the lists be open, the poems laid on the line.
Before my EYE OF THE NEEDLE, his skill shall not prevail,
Though he try to make me sodden with gallons of WILD GRAPE WINE,
And set his CARIBOO HORSES on my tail.

Oh I can't wait to visit the igloo of the soul
Where Acorns, Birneys, Newloves, and bards of equal fame
Have plastered both themselves and every leaking hole

And warmed their hearts at PURDY's flame.

Kate Braid

SAY THE NAMES
after Al Purdy

Say abrasive.
Say abatjour, abutment and adze eye.
Say aggregate and air-dried cement, say
alabaster anchor blocks, anhydrous lime and
antemion. Say apprentice, with an arabesque.
Say arris at the place two edges meet and
eyes up to the architrave of the door
and the artisan who built it.
Say ashlar and auger, avoirdupois and azimuth.
Now bridge to badigeon and ball peen,
to beams and barefaced tenons.
Embrace barefoot joints and bargeboards,
bezel and batter board.
Chant bay, bead and reel and bead and butt molding,
bell-hanger's bit.
Belay us a benchmark, bevel to bias.
Don't stop now—say bleeding tile, blind mortise,
block and tackle. Bring on board and batten, bolts
and bond stones.
Then there's buck and built-up beams and
burl, butt hinge and still
we're only on the b's because this building,
this building is concrete bloody poetry, please!

Magie Dominic

STANDING ON A NEWFOUNDLAND CLIFF
(Inspired by "Trees at the Arctic Circle")

The breeze had changed to a robust wind,
I could feel it across my shoulders. It was rushing the clouds.

Waves below were crashing on ancient stones
that were long ago torn from the cliffs;
sea foam littered the beach.

The sky was bursting with colors I'd never seen in my life.
Mauve and cerise and splashes of charcoal
crisscrossed the sky like chalk marks left by a child.
The air felt like silver.

Wind raged around me and ripped through the tuckamore trees,
those swirling dervishes that inhabit the tops
of Newfoundland cliffs,
branches and limbs gone wild,
outliving the elements.

Tuckamores are unique to Newfoundland;
they challenge torturous storms
and the waves crashing below them;
defy the wind and its violence,
and when denied the chance to grow upward,
in an act of survival and daring,
they simply grow sideways.

I stood alone at the top of the cliff that day,
waves crashing below,
a furious wind engulfing me and the tuckamores,
and I inhaled their courage and daring.
I reclaimed a part of myself.

I devoured a piece of the cliff that day;
a taste of wildness and strength; of vastness;
of forest and storms.
Alchemy.

Bruce Cockburn

3 AL PURDYS

Stand in the swaying boxcar doorway
moving east away from the sunset and
after a while the eyes digest a country and
the belly perceives a mapmaker's vision
in dust and dirt on the face and hands here
its smell drawn deep through the nostrils down
to the lungs and spurts through the bloodstream
campaigns in the lower intestine and
chants love songs to the kidneys
After a while there is no arrival and
no departure possible any more
you are where you were always going
and the shape of home is under your fingernails.

I'm a product of some parents of the sort that shouldn't breed
didn't get much schooling past learning how to read
got the poetry bug in some forgotten institution
when first I did embark on my career of destitution
the beauty of language set a hook in my soul
me like a breadcrust soaking soup from a bowl
You can call this a rant but I declare I declaim
Al Purdy's poems are the name of the game
the winds of fate blow where they will
I'll give you 3 Al Purdy's for a twenty dollar bill

Porkers in the counting house counting out the bacon
matter's getting darker in the universe they're making
they love the little guy until they get a better offer
with the dollar getting smaller they can fit more in their coffers
and the doings on the corner neither sung nor seen
they're circling the shopping carts at Sherbourne and Queen
I resemble that assembly but I'm not the same

Al Purdy's poems are the name of my game
the winds of fate blow where they will
I'll give you 3 Al Purdy's for a twenty dollar bill

You can spit on the prophet but respect the word
I've got some lines I want to spin you that you ought to have heard
the winds of fate blow where they will
I'll give you 3 Al Purdy's for a twenty dollar bill

the winds of fate blow where they will
I'll give you 3 Al Purdy's for a twenty dollar bill

And after the essence of everything
had exchanged itself for words and became
another being and could even be summoned
from the far distance we chanted a spell of names
and we said "mountain be our friend"
and we said "River guard us from enemies"
And we said what it seemed the gods themselves
might say if we had dreamed them and they
had dreamed us from their high places
and they spoke to us in the forest
from the river and the mountain
and the mouths of the ochre-painted dead
had speech again and the waters
spoke and the speech had words
and our children remembered

Kath MacLean

SPRING AT ROBLIN LAKE

Speaking sharply, her voice rising to a hiss, Wind cursed Spring for her late arrival. All night she wailed. By morning, trees were covered in spit. Buds that might have bloomed, curled into themselves, maples, branches heavy with snow, sagged & leaning towards the little cottage, were suddenly old—

Caught in the bramble, thorns pricked, lines were drawn; limbs cast about— there were casualties, *yes*. Twigs, leaves, breezy bombs circled round the shed, flung
the outhouse door open, beat it senseless. Cedars aching with loss bent in prayer, but what to pray?

Forgiveness,
mercy,
Love?

No man's land. Raphael wounded, offered no resolution, no comfort, no joy—

Lilacs, tender & fair, huddled by the drive, quivering, faded from mauve to white. Swans blessed the lake, caressed its silken cheek, then in a flurry of feathers were gone. Dog found curses in the grass, crushed, misshapen, forgotten nuts, dried shells, September's spent leaves & other mementos of the living dead. Wind swayed, & snapping the tulips' yellow heads, choked the poetic, strangled Romanticism, blew a breath of beer caps from the Quinte—

Footnotes to a forgotten story: warmer climes, summer stars, young love, songbirds singing—But robins don't sing & sparrows choking, cough a note or two. Herons on spindly legs beat their wings against the light until morning's eyes shine black. The day undone, seeds scatter on the back deck, pods. What might have been long ago, no longer means—

Horses, dogs, a marten sniffs beneath my window, follows what can't be seen: messages from beyond, air, a whispering statue, a girl turned stone. Lifting the cottage, separating earth, rock, fall face first into Roblin Lake, surface in the moment, then claw about the edges of shore. Dead, or alive, blessing Night, who gives close encounters, with things, people, *things*—

Refuse the ending. Tipping the A-frame: water, weeds, fishes, silt—redirect heaven & Raphael's swinging feet—

Thoughts crawl through the gables, squirrels scratch my wasp-infested skin, everything itches. Barn boards swarm with swallows, old souls, still—longing for voice: alphabet, omega, words might speak to the woman in the portrait, converse with these shadows; whose hand rises, falls, burns this green stick?

Winter, spring, day, night; the marten scratches at the window. Dog & I asleep in the cottage, in the A-frame on Roblin Lake—this seasonless season; Al smokes a cigar & the war seems endless—

Lynn Tait

CHALLENGING THE LAW OF SUPERIMPOSITION

and I am angry remembering
remembering the song of flesh
to flesh and bone to bone
the loss is better
—Al Purdy, *"Listening to Myself"*

I had no poem to write, nothing to offer,
though buried speechless in the same landscape
brought me closer to him.
In his place, my space, the land speaks—
childhood memories ingrained with visual clues.
After a 20-year absence, I walk through woods behind my house,
find my secret hideaways, the quarry, even the raspberry patch;
everything as I left it, only taller,
and I am angry remembering.

Too young. Too young
to travel, what seemed great distances alone.
Family car rides weaving through back-roads—Hastings,
Prince Edward County—it was all the same to me.
I was the Canadian Shield—a geological landmark that did not belong,
leaving chatter marks in places that should not exist,
a fossil even then, and when I reach his grave site,
we enter a convergent boundary—two landmasses
remembering the song of flesh,

the lyric leaching out,
purple milk under my skin,
creeping towards each other
like his blue heron shifts along thin rivers,
closer and closer, flesh
to flesh and bone to bone.

Reading his poems now, swear I was by his side—
know his nurse log, have seen the golden apples
abandoned and white capped.
And though hear *his* Nature's sighs and calls
and think of death often,
prefer to remember him hung over,
slugging back coffee in downtown Trenton,
rather than a renewable resource.
The loss is better.

Purdy Country Literary Festival, 2009

Steven Heighton

MAPS OF THE TOP OF THE WORLD

New moon—a starveling
  curled on blue earth and quickly
    swallowed by snowdrift clouds—

Late in *The Lure of the Labrador Wild*
the solemn falling of snow in the firwood, the
famine-wood, and before long sly, soft winds,
till drifts oversift the tomb of the tent
like an A-frame in a snowbelt storm

—and inside that canvas husk
a smaller husk now exempt from struggle, the ardent
anomalies of consciousness, animal heat
and shunted blood. Sink now sleep a fugue
of crackling maps, wistful misnamings echoing
in talus-grey defiles—

> Providence Point
> Cape Homer
> Homeward Cove—

                              of firepits
once more warmly
antlered with flame.
                    The explorer's dream
is just the yearning of doomed
molecules for eternity, ancient urge
to impregnate barrens with menhirs,
cairns and runes, with
ruins,

    and you there likewise,
                    Purdy,

in your oxygen tent,
                    mind off elsewhere
                                   stumbling in a blizzard
of drugs—

                 you too came this far,
     imprinted the ice shelves and foolscap floes
of how many blank sheets
and pharmacy notebooks,
                              wanted to "do the country"
so you kept afoot, always moving
against the stasis to come, always
talking back at the silence to come

                                   and that final forecloser,
repossessor, who serves the body
such intimate writs, gives pressing notice
each breath is borrowed, the warmed and
wobbling space you occupy
is leased—

And maybe all this movement and exploration is really
in hopes of finding—founding—some new "Vinland
the Good"
                 somewhere out beyond
all vital eviction, where poets, friends,
like dogged squatters in life's rickety A-frame
vie and recite over homebrew, wild grape wine,
with invincible livers on a pine-box patio
that never will sag further than this

—and the day holds, hovering at the late August hour
of light's most inebriate angle, on the relic
phonograph Paul Robeson revived to the lap
and backbeat of lake-waves, woodwind breezes
through the weeping willow's green marquee,

and the old rowboat is straked and caulked so that later
a few might row it across to the brook mouth
and alongside the pioneer graveyard, knowing
its bottomless appetite is finally sated
and the living forever barred....

He loved the poetry of place-names most
and set them down accordingly—

So sink now sleep a fugue
of crackling maps, wistful misnamings
signposted in permafrost

> Ft Good Hope
> Mt Somerset
> Pt Victory

the pit of the belly
once again warmly
furnaced with flame,

> and "know where the words came from"

Christine Smart

STONE SONG

> *in the river's white racket*
> *the shore trembles*
> *like a stone song*
> —Al Purdy

A pall descends
a long shadow without end—
the slant of light on a mountain,
a snaking ochre tree, wet with rain
> *in the river's white racket.*

Illumination itself, warm as the sun in summer,
the body no longer a boat, a vehicle, a fluid
instrument except for three breaths
lying still, open and floating
> *the shore trembles.*

The river cascades, pain ebbs
and fades, limbs soften
and dissolve. The flowers sound
like bells and I am free
> *like a stone song.*

Solveig Adair

LAMENT FOR A SMALL TOWN

in beginning darkness / at the end of hunger
—Al Purdy, "Lament for the Dorsets"

they find a small doll
hand stitched, a roll of copper
wire cradled by
a rotting wagon the house
already sinking
into the forest's regrowth

the plates were on the
table—food too old to rot

it was like they sat
for lunch and were distracted
by the whistle of
the train which no longer stopped
fading out midbite
disappearing with their town

no roads on that side
of the river the railway
the artery that
suddenly vanished, starving
the town into nothing

these ghosts, these dead dreams
appear sometimes in pictures
people and buildings
frozen into the land's bones

we will not keep them
in our own dreams and stories
no thousand years of
myth to give life to these dead

the last man in town
crawled out from his decaying
house, his decaying
body to the train that no
longer stopped they found
him lying across the tracks
or so the station
master says when he's drinking

that last man his wife
and child dead as the old town
no place to travel
and the old cart rotting out
making not a meal
but a burnt offering to
empty chairs and hearts

leaving a small doll against
the telegraph line
that never came arteries
slowly cutting off
as he crawled out into the
sun

Karen Solie

THE SHARING ECONOMY

This performance of
"I Want My Fucking Money"
broadcast live from the street will conclude
when the last human being on earth
has perished.

The Freshly Renovated Bachelor Suite has its ear
to the ground, has the ear
of the Paying Guest
who's found a bed down there among
the learning experiences
and automatic functions,
decor objects from HomeSense's
Blunt Force Trauma Collection

above which the house hovers like a spaceship
in a super-convenient location
and the Hosts walk overland.

A pilot light flickers
like an awareness of self,
chaos whispering through the fittings,

pipes singing, patterns
in the textiles repeating, the weeping tile—

between sound and silence
is music.

The Paying Guest rises in the middle of the night
to turn off the radio where no radio exists,

a disturbance imminent over the sea—no
the lake—
it will come clear in a minute.

The furnace knocks twice
then hesitates, and the Paying Guest
lying in the lettings
remembers the old joke about the drummer
and now the Paying Guest is laughing on the inside.

John Oughton

LONG REACH: THANKSGIVING, 2000

for Al Purdy

In placed, willow-dragged waters
of the Long Reach
a muskrat swims on its back
human as myself on holiday
working at doing nothing: it
is just as true that I, floating on
my back, water rilling off whiskers,
recall the muskrat's
climbing cells shelved
in the library of my genes.

As it drags Quinte Bay water along,
my course makes the smallest echo
of a southbound duck flight's V

And I backswim 40 years ago
where no muskrat or man
in right mind floated here,
because gentlemanly Bob Hayward,
clean white shirt and tie,
was beating back Yankee hydroplanes
with beautiful *Miss Supertest*,
her supercharged 16-cyclinder Rolls-Royce Griffon
powering polished wood up to 160 mph
kicking up a rooster tail tall as six-story
buildings that, thank God, still aren't
along the Long Reach.

Now *Miss Supertest* hangs
in the Ontario Science Centre, her roar

shrunk to a single plaque, memento
mori of Bob Hayward barrel-rolling to death
on the Detroit River and
Supertest gas stations, those odd little castle
keeps of Canada's internal combustion cult
are extinct as Fina, and your body from this life,
Al Purdy. The mystery of how water becomes fire.

Some poor dumb herbivorous dinosaur
two hundred million years ago reached
for tender branches just a little
too far over the pond and went in.
Time cooked her down
to high-test fuel hammering
Miss Supertest's stressed, polished pistons
rhythmic as big Canadian presses pumping
out Al Purdy poetry books
which taught me to see
timewise, my eye extending
not only the facts of the past,
but the emotions that pool in a place
sung by local ghosts
buried inside the green dissembling
of goldenrod, milkweed and
caterpillar, all of them wanting.

Wanting made matter
spell out a nucleus, then gild it with scales.
Wanting inspired a fish mocked by slimy neighbours
to go walkabout on fins,
made me contemplate this
Long Reach deadhead that becomes
a muskrat's head examining me.

Who is further along the scale
of evolving? I who want so much

in both senses—desire and lack?
This muskrat who wants nothing
and slips underwater
before I can interrogate him.
Just another Hermes in a slinky fur suit,
one of many messengers the world
shoves in my face, urging
"Pay attention, fool!"

It's in that silence
that the 16 cylinders of thought
power up a rooster tail of words.
Call it poetry if a term is needed
or nature talking:
me just the mouthpiece,
a ripple on the surface,
and gone.

Glen Sorestad

CACTUS CATHEDRAL

remembering Al Purdy

The poet betakes himself into the desert
accompanied only by the morning breeze to enact the daily rite
of purging his bowels of the previous day's excesses,
picking his prudent way amongst a mute choir of cacti,
diverse in shapes and sizes—barrel, prickly pear, dagger
and pincushion, lechuguilla and yucca—lurking
like a minefield to punish his stumble or misstep.

At the designated site, he locates the technology
of the desert crapper, seizes in one firm hand the lawn chair
with toilet seat firmly affixed, while the other grasps
the long-handled spade, a scepter orbed with a toilet tissue roll.
Thus equipped, he strolls off to his own seclusion
to meditate on desert life while the sun creeps above
the Chisos Mountains. Although the poet is no Muslim,
nor even a practising Christian, he turns the lawn chair
to watch the February sun begin its morning crawl.

He begins his communion with the morning breeze
in this cathedral of spines and prickles, but his mind
fastens on the possibility of lurking beasts—an aggressive coyote
darting from behind a yucca to snap at his bared buttocks;
or a cougar come down from the mountains; or a pack of javelinas
drawn to the noxious fragrance as to one of their own,
then turning on the intruder like outraged parishioners
routing out a promiscuous pastor.

But here, in the Chihuahuan desert, the poet ruminates,
undisturbed, by anything but his own thoughts, and now,
his rites concluded, he buries his offering, leaving no evidence
of his passing, hole filled in, desert left unsullied.

He returns spade and chair to their former location,
gingerly picks his way, rejuvenated, towards the climbing sun.

Kath MacLean

TOO TALL FOR ANTIQUITY

Sometimes it just
rains.

& the river rising, swells,
draws in its breath & falling,
dreams its drowned thoughts.

Bubbles rise to the surface. Frothing,
the lake laughs.
(You are laughing too) I think

before—
yesterday's dandelions breathless
& seedy, poke about the grass,
stems of nothing ask
for a poem as if—

Listen, I say,
grass ripples by the lake,
rocks cradle a ragged shore. Where
I sleep a kaleidoscope:
ash & berry branches, leaves
stroke your face in the bark of a willow,
watching—

Weeds rub green to green.
A mating dance, a swish of swan,
shade, & feathers beat
about the beach.

Pebbles, small thoughts
from your chair. Rain

fogs the sky without matches, without
light. Neighbours burn
sheaves of poems. Shelley's wind,
although well-spoken, doesn't
speak to me or
I don't listen.

Careful, mice frantic for freedom;
cry in their steel traps. I let them
go and one by one they come back.
Knives, forks, spoons in the drawers fill
with their nightly visits. Yours, more
quiet, slip by the shadows, spit
in the fire
hiss & burn—

Each day is
as it is in the rain.

Thistles along the drive noisy
& prickling interrupt—
What did you say?

Eurithe tells me classics need rereading.
Prometheus wanders looking for light,
turns on the hall switch, & stumbling
all thumbs, is useless
to fetch a pail of water,
or catch the drip drip under the door
umbrella finds so funny.

Trojans fill the house with rain,
& spill golden apples on the floor.
Bruised, the season turns. Dandelions,
wheels of the world, spin when Spring rises
to the tips of her toes, hovers

by the window as if she might grow too big
for box-books, too tall for antiquity.

Head spinning, the ceiling sways,
the hanged man's noose tightens
the knot. I bend at the knees & pray
for a miracle, a small thought
fills my head—

The screech of a boiling kettle.
Tea, for two I say.
Dogchild agrees.
There is promise;
there is this. Small breath,
this seed of a poem.

Unaccustomed to speaking, chair
squeaks as I shift my hips close
to the window a robin turns
as surprised to see me
as I am it.

& the rain keeps
& the pails fill
& you are
in the tree a poem
as far as far
       as antiquity—

Peter Trower

THE LAST SPAR-TREE ON ELPHINSTONE MOUNTAIN
for Al Purdy

The last spar-tree on Elphinstone Mountain
through drunken-Sunday binoculars
pricks the blue bubble of the sky
on that final ridge where the scar tissue peters out.

Been four years quiet now on the battered mountain's back
except for shakecutters, hunters and stray philosophers.
The trucks are elsewhere; some of the drivers dead
and the donkeys gone to barber another hill.

I'm always shooting my mouth off about mountains
sometimes climbing them
and sometimes just distantly studying them like this.
My eyes need no caulk boots
I can vault to that ridge in my mind,
stand at the foot of that tree, forlorn as a badly used woman
become merely landmark and ravenperch.
I can touch its bark sunwarm as flesh
feel the engines still shaking it functional
with vibrations that never quite die.

It's either a cornfield or a catastrophe.
Either a crop or a tithe or a privacy
has been taken from this place.
What matter? It's done. Beyond that ridge is a valley
I helped hack and alter. There's a gully there
three hundred feet deep in places
where we tailholted on its rim.
Dizzy abyss that scared the wits out of me

you furrow down the mountain like God's own drainage ditch
and stopped a forest fire in 1965.

At your foot is the dirtiest show of them all
where we logged in the box canyon with debris crashing down
and the rotten hemlock snags trembled over us,
the haulback stumps pulled out like bad teeth.
The hooktender said: "She's a natural-born bitch!"
The lines broke—the omens spoke
and I quit from fear to become a brief boomman.

I'm getting melodramatic again but it's hard not to.
Logging's larger than life. Keep your sailors and cowboys!
I'm always stressing the sombre side
but there was much of comradeship and laughter—
great yarns beside noon donkeys; hillhumour between turns,
excellent shits behind stumps with the wind fanning the stink away,
sweat smelling good and cigarette smoke celestial.

Dream on in peace, old tree—
perhaps you're a truer monument to man
than any rocktop crucifix in Rio De Janeiro.

Autumn Richardson

WHEN THE DEITIES ARE TENDED, MORNING COMES

I see the curvature of the earth
its great bent back

wind-sore pines and juniper
crouched into stone.

Stars roost in high darkness.

All here bend to the elements
and so do I

leaning into fire, tending coals—
this is the altar and I offer

the sun's cells, excised from cedar
and birch, joints of driftwood

"become the heat of my blood
the sap of my lips"

smoke blooms, antiseptic, alterative

enters the cavities of my body
the pores of the forest

mingles with the violet notes
of coyote, who comes in close.

Jeanette Lynes

ROADTRIPPING

to a Kingston ex

I can tell you now that you're not listening
why I stayed: because it was like living
inside an Al Purdy poem. Good grief
we drove, didn't we, that country
north of Belleville as it disappeared
before our eyes and like any
self-respecting man you refused
to ask for directions when we got lost.
And you could build anything
from scrap lumber. You were handy.
A Purdy sort of guy. You wouldn't
give up when we couldn't find
the Quinte Hotel, even after the locals
said it burnt down. *It's in a poem*, I insisted
so it must exist. The locals looked at me
funny but you defended my insistence
and remember the man in Marmora,
famous for his dragonfly photographs?
You also drove me to lilac forests
so I could quote "May 23, 1980."
You liked the barroom brawl poem best—
a man who could stand up for poetry
and still be a man, even though poems
won't buy a goddam thing. But now
I must *also* say those "north of 7" jokes
got old fast and you laughed a *bit*
too heartily and anyway, they
weren't in the poems. They were life
imitating life.

Rachel Rose

IOWA CITY

for the writers of IWP 2015

Tell me, do the cicadas sing in your country?
Here the trees whose names I do not know
tremble with the voltage of their music.
Here we gather to compare the suffering of our people.
Tell me, do monarch butterflies fall from the sky
in your country? I saw one yesterday, walking
along a sidewalk at the edge of the gleaming river,
wings ragged as the flags of invaded countries.

A butterfly walking is a sad thing. Perhaps this one
had seen the newspaper whose pages blew
in endless circles at the corner where the bridge meets
the earth, the same bad news lifting briefly,
then dropped again by invisible hands.

I live on the western tip of a northern country,
too cold for cicadas, too far west for monarch butterflies.
Don't speak to me about politics. Once I had answers,
but even when I did, people gathered in the squares of the world
with candles, with children on their shoulders, and were shot down.
Now my questions are butterflies walking.

Now, writers, when we sit together
under the nameless throbbing trees
to read the book of our lives aloud
to one another, I feel the red joy of the cardinal
at riverside, another bird unfamiliar as this heartland landscape.

In rooms too small to hold our great desire to connect,
the Nigerian writer asks to be translated to Chinese,
and his wish is granted; the Brazilian writer

who expects to be lonely with his Portuguese
discovers he was never alone.

I tell you, before we leave this place,
I will shape my mouth to Spanish verse,
I will dream in Arabic, hold the acrid smoke
of Cairo and Ulaanbaatar in my lungs
as we stand together in the only permitted place
for writers to exhale. We will breathe each other in
and Northern Lights will burn in each of you.

Ben Ladouceur

STOCKPILE

I think the time for fires has begun.
For constant fires: a depletion time.
I have less taste than ever for these ghosts.
If I can see my breath when I wake up,
I put this place behind me and come home.

You mustn't fall in love with logs. A log
is gone the day its tree bursts from its seed.
A log is unfelt fire for decades. Then,
you start the fire. You feel the fire. That's life.
That's logs. My father chopped the wood for me.

That's life too. When you're born, you only love
the woman. So the man must earn his love
as my father earned his. With a blue axe.
While I sat in the cabin, writing this.

Dymphny Dronyk

ODE TO AL PURDY—A LITTER OF POETS

Walking the puppy amid the ruins
of another long winter, lawns sepia with mould,
the snow dying without grace, gumbo on my heels,
the dog is happy, her tail a flag of joy
but I curse this exile north of 55
and the circumpolar wind, ugly as seal breath,
that haunts a landscape unfit for anyone
but skittish trappers or a priest
on the verge of being defrocked.

T.S. Eliot was right—this is the cruellest month.
Litter thrusts out of the snow
like a thousand rude gestures
and I long for the tsunami of green
that is April on the West Coast.
But this morning my mother insisted
she was not crazy, there was a robin perched
on her steaming compost box
and so I listen for bird song and follow
my small white wolf, who unlike me
is bred for a lifetime in Siberia.

Then, there in the snow bank
brazen as strippers, blinking in the sun,
a posse of beer bottles,
trapped mid cheers.
I freeze, entranced by the arctic blue
of the label, a silver effigy of the Kokanee glacier
that defined the horizon where I grew up.
I think of my friend Tom
who wrote a poem about his friend Al

and beer bottles as prairie crocuses
and endless highways and hope.

Suddenly I am elated
as I stagger on with the dog,
drunk with joy that it is April,
that I can call myself Canadian, a citizen of
a country of countries, of 13 solitudes,
where a poet drinks beer at school
and throws the empties out his office window
and is not only forgiven but celebrated,
where the geese over my head chant
about the typewriter ribbon highways
they've traced back to this still-empty north.

A country where poets
work their lines in factories,
where poets weld stanzas at Syncrude,
where in April poets thumb our noses
at cruelty and spring blizzards,
pack a sack of beer into the trunk
and head out on the road with the geese.
A country where poetry is not
the only place that truth is spoken,
where we may still speak truth
and be forgiven.

The dog glances up at my laughter
her eye as blue as an ice chip,
and I tell her I am drunk too
with reverence for the voyageur poets
who shaped our collective voice,
the big footsteps
in which I am walking,
where words stumble along with me,

in love with this land
and its April pussy willows,
the coyote trails through my small city
and the vast aching wealth
of distance that unites us
from coast to coast to coast.

Autumn Richardson

CHRYSALIDS

Following the curves of Salem
Road:

a thin bleed of sumac through ditches
and thick November woods all the colours
of a coyote's back

countless barns leaning, splitting;
clay-blue, faded green paints flaking
into winter-white fields

trees are nearly leafless;
their sap-pulses slow; they're spooling
inwards, becoming slim overwintering
chrysalids.

At the edge of Roblin Lake heron arrives
as calligraphy each evening.

All the voices of morning—cicadas,
crickets, tree-frogs—have vanished.

Ian Williams

GROUND RULES

Let's begin with
Do not microwave caribou head.
I am told the eyes will explode.

Do not hunt or microwave polar bears.
Same reason.

My homeroom teacher
who had a nervous breakdown
said we should not pee on the walls.
We hadn't been, as far as I know.
But I feel that should be on record here.

Do not microwave robin eggs. Do not
microwave Johnny Cash songs. At any time
do not microwave the terror by night
nor the arrow that flieth by day.

Did I—yes—don't hunt polar bears.
No reason.

Do not microwave the Arctic
or the Rockies because my doctor friend takes all
of March off to ski. He's quite quiet. He is quietly
avalanching. So you don't want to cross him.

Do not microwave turbo prop planes
as they take off. Or memories of people you love.
Or the memories of. A thousand shall fall
at thy side, and ten thousand at thy right hand;
but it shall not come nigh thee. Thou shalt not
microwave the sun.

Cornelia Hoogland

AL DEVELOPS HIS PLEASURES

Al's arm was amputated,
this made him so miserable he got
a species reassignment.
He grew four legs. Became a horse.
Immediately his friends wanted a ride.
Whoa! he said. He wanted to develop his new
identity slowly, wasn't sure what his equine pleasures
involved. Movement and speed?
A concern for the terrain? Blinkhorn Trail,
for example, involved too much footwork.
As for his love life, he was the only horse around.
This concerned him. And Eurithe.
She scrolled obscure websites
for combs to curry his backside in a way she hoped
was pleasurable, and yes, she noticed
he twitched his mane, half-closed his big eyes.
Or should she post an ad, find him a more suitable mate?
It wasn't clear if the change was permanent
or transitory—how much effort should she, or he, invest?
Corralled in his horse flesh, what could he do,
people saying, Let's go see Al who's become a horse,
and cracking horse jokes. A horse walks into a bar,
the bartender asks why the long face?
Al might have explained, but all that came out
was a whinny. And his friends only wanted rides.
Al didn't budge, he stood there, sniffing the air.

Ken Babstock

CROMWELL'S HEAD UNDER THE ANTECHAPEL

Under a standing back-to-work order,
each leaning in to their angle grinder,
the cicadas of Empire Loyalist country
react to a splatter film live-streamed
on a windscreen.

"Windscreen?"—shield. One local birder
from Wellington, or lone hoarder, or Auditor
of the College of Silver, scans between-channel poplars
for rock peplars, tits, bobble-link bracelets, lost kites
and induced seizures.

He's had enough of quiz night. Crests, crosses,
pubs, and Elizabeth's, he's had enough of. His rebus
has "Basta" over Malevich's black square. A low float
plane burps across the left aural quadrant
and all extant

literature on voluntary statelessness
compresses to lake lap in a lab's ear. One tosses
one's hat in the air at the ends of wars. One guesses.
Senses are a sickness here at the core, the corn,
the Cornwall Report.

Pendant lamps are a kitchen's super moon,
which is to say light never gets closer or noon
is home's apposite and frightening adjustor.
We murdered years with knives pry-barred
in toasters. These are cowbirds.

LEGACY

Phil Hall

from ESSAY ON LEGEND

Most days Al Purdy

wrote poems as good as Alden Nowlan
    but maybe 30 times Al wrote a poem we now call   a Purdy poem

as if some days his name were All   not Al

    Nowlan also   at times   sawdust flying   achieved a wider name
All-Done-Now Land   or Old In No Land

    they both wrote a lot of friendly crap that sounds the same

if read now   but who can stand to read them exhaustively now
    they were drinkers   & that will get a soul above itself some

as the booze digs under eloquence like surf

    but Purdy seems to have   seen & heard   his over-self
he caricatured Al as All   or was that us

    while Nowlan just kept writing down memories & impressions

without distinguishing small-town small-talk from the bull moose secret life
    so we tend to forget him

Otty Lake, 2016

Kat Cameron

HOW STUDENTS IMAGINE THE DORSETS

> *they have never imagined us in their future*
> *how could we imagine them in the past*
> —Al Purdy, "Lament for the Dorsets"

I thought it was a simple poem
      a few remnants of the past—*tent rings, carved ivory swans*—
a forgotten people, reimagined.
        I forgot how uninformed my students are
           living in their solipsistic world.

Giants are important to storytelling.
      Sometimes I want to weep
at their ignorance. The poem
      is not a fairytale. The Dorsets
        were not giants.

Back then people had nothing
      and they had to survive in the wilderness.
True, in our glutted apartments, we cannot imagine the poverty
      of a people who survived on seal meat
        in *a caribou-skin tent.*

In "Lament" Purdy uses Canadian history to exaggerate
        the negative viewpoint on settlers invading Dorset land.
No. Indoctrinated into the colonial mindset,
        they can't imagine that the *little men*
        who came from the west with dogs,
the men who pushed out the Dorsets, were Inuit,
        not settlers.

If the ivory swan can survive, so can the people in this poem.
      Ye Gods, it's a lament. They're all dead. Extinct. Gone.

How to explain extinction to a twenty-year-old student?
       Death has not entered their world.
They cannot imagine a tent in the frozen Arctic,
          where one old man carves
              his memories into ivory swans.

Purdy writes,
      I have been stupid in a poem.
But this poet who left school at 17,
      an autodidact who wrote about
Cuba, China, Greece, and Ameliasburg, Ontario,
      Arctic trees, Plato's cave,
         imagines worlds he has never seen,
           carvers and hunters who live again.
Piecing together stories—
      poets piece together the fragments left behind.

John B. Lee

THE UNVEILING

i

I'm on my way
to an unveiling
the great poet
has been turned to stone

ii

in a bar
we raise a glass
mine is
dark ale
I remember
how the poet
whose statue
we have just
honoured
was here
with us in 87
raising a pint
to another friend
only then
a few days dead
and I saw
my face
in the looking glass
and joked

"oh, see there
they've hung

our picture
over the bar"
and three of us
look and laugh
to see ourselves
a pigeon
on each head
dove-shouldered
immortalized in white.

iii

at the unveiling
the shy couple
polish the poet
like the bathing of the dead
a week
in the sun
and he's too tarnished
for ceremony
the mayor, the living laureate
the benefactor
all want *shine*
a week ago
installed by crane
the poet
hanged by the neck
came down
from the sky
to land on the slab circumference
of a grass-flat plinth
suspended
on the makeshift gallows
hung, as it were, for the crime of silence
a girl

climbed onto his lap
before the wax was set
two students
stopped and shouted
"that's Al Purdy!"
and then, today, after the rubbing
the sheet dropped down
to drape his frame
and we drank
away an hour
as I wondered
"what is happening under the sheet?"
in the ripple
of the wind-stirred shroud

iv

his widow
touched by light
stood in the shade
of the life-like one-and-one-half-sized man
with whom she had shared
a bed
she reached out, briefly
caressed his black-marble calf
the crowd
let out a sigh
like wing-breath on a single shade of green
her mind alone
inheld
the meaning of that touch.

Jeanette Lynes

ENGLISH ASSIGNMENT: SITUATE AL PURDY'S POEMS IN THEIR VARIOUS LITERARY TRADITIONS

The graveyard tradition
The tradition of fallen fence poems
Barroom brawl poems, hold your horses poems
Horse poems, rural party line poems
Mice in the house poems
Sestinas on train poems
Sick poems
Impermanent husband poems
Jackhammer poems
Anecdote poems
Argument poems
Gospel poems
Houseguest from hell poems
With all due respect poems
With no respect poems
Open road poems
Dead car battery poems
Neolithic skull poems
Starling poems
Island dream poems
Dude poems
Poems about Ms. Atwood
Say the names poems
The tradition of poems that allows cussing
And if there's no tradition of cosmic
ass-kicking poems
there damned well is now

Rob Taylor

ON REALIZING EVERYONE HAS WRITTEN SOME BAD POEMS

Another poem starts poorly, ends with pangs
of shame which cause my hands to reach out
like Purdy's hands snatching up loose copies of *The Enchanted
Echo* to later burn, or not (a good legend's never clear).

I read my poem and it bitters on my tongue
like the baking powder my father packed in pancakes
he poured and served out to us (unknowingly?) half-
cooked each early Sunday morning 'til his death.

I think of Purdy in his A-Frame, midwinter,
low on firewood, a row of *Echo*es fading on the shelf.
Maybe he reached out his hands and grabbed them.
Maybe he let them be. I don't care which.

The choice matters, to be sure, splits hero from fool,
but it matters far less than its making.

Sid Marty

THE STATUE OF AL PURDY

The Statue of Al Purdy unveiled
that day in Toronto, felt wrong,
seeing the complex man
I had come to know
composed, forever, in one mode.

I should have been forewarned
to see Al Purdy turned to bronze.

To me he seemed more often
poised to spring, like a mountain lion,
an active man who'd throw
a big paw around you and growl
"Let's talk about those poems
you sent me." (Or sometimes, not.)

Yet skepticism made him question
formal compliments betimes,
as if they compromised
his blue collar style.
So the sculptors got it right,
leaving out the jacket and tie.

Eurithe Purdy, age 84,
had dragged herself from hospital
to be there, and after the speechifying
bid them pull the veil aside,
but damned if it didn't fall right over her,
So she struggled under the canvas
for air, in a scary cartoon.

Say what you want about Toronto,
but nobody laughed as we rescued
Al's muse from the fallout
of his great honour,
a glitch that might have levelled
a weaker old-timer.

I asked Jim Purdy what he thought
of it all and Jim, built on a Purdy frame,
with his father's voice to match
rumbled, "Well, I don't recall
the beatific smile."

I'd like to think Al
might have said exactly that.

But friend Ruth Harvey remembers
an edge of hubris in the voice
of that insouciant Everyman one time,
when Al, his feet hanging out the window
of the Purdy land-ship to cool, challenged
a puzzled yokel with, "Do you know who I am?"
then muttered, "Well, it doesn't matter."

And once, in my wife's café in Pincher Creek
with the Purdys sitting there
we could not find one customer who'd heard of him.
Angered, Myrna hissed "Do you realize who he is?"

But that was Pincher Creek,
a town named after a pair of pliers.

Now his statue answers the question
for anybody wandering by:
"The Voice of the Land."

Well, I guess I'm glad it's there,
though I prefer the human voice
to the noble inscription.

Still, I wonder if the author
of *The Cariboo Horses,*
wrangler to the wild horses of poetry
might "Cast a cold eye"
even on that sincere depiction,

as if Al Purdy ever could be
frozen in fiction.

Willow Valley, Alberta, 2017

Doug Paisley

ROBLIN LAKE

Where I shouldn't be
Wearing someone else's coat
This place doesn't want me
Or I don't want to be here
Asking so little of myself
Chainsaws are running across the lake
And I'm too timid to fart
Too conspicuous on the road
And I slept too late
Let the time sail by
Tried to enjoy a smoke and a beer
What kind of person tries to enjoy that?
Pick up the phone put down the phone
Let the food spoil
Let the fire die
Couldn't sit still
What's original here? people asked
I guess I don't know
Saw a chip bowl from an old photograph
Up on a shelf
That wall looks too white and new
That chair could be from back then
20, 30, 50 years ago
Who doesn't want to turn away from today
And picture all those struggles that resolved
or just ended?

My infant son for one
This place with no toys
A heron on the shore he'd like to chase
Its murky, skeletal presence
No sinew on the bone

Of scribbles in books and luggage tags
Shelves of cobweb spines
Where once a path was hacked
Through forests of words unpublished
Skirting glades of certainty
To build a home rough and unruly
Sending lines arcing through the sweetest point
That draws our minds' own words
Like no song, no siren
And lay down by the millpond with a culminating sigh
That swallowed everything

Howard White

THE POET'S WIFE

for Eurithe Purdy

For fifty years her role was to be the brake
On a runaway imagination
Also to put up with a lot of crap
In the name of art (poverty, infidelity, anonymous toil)
Now that she is fifteen years alone it is different
She has become the keeper of that flame
That once gave her so much anguish
She is the one left to make the case
For that bewildering and troubling journey
She found her life carried away on
And poetry, the strange obsession
That gripped her otherwise prosaic man
Has become the focus of her nostalgia
As she recollects the work she always left to him
Realizing that she is now in some ways
Its best and only witness and advocate
People press her constantly to interpret and explain
That work she always left to others
And slowly she discovers she knows it
After all with a lived-in authority
No one on earth can match
She knows the desolation and horror
That lay behind some of those sweet lines
She knows something nobody else could know
About how poetry is formed from life
Like the pearl that hides the oyster's pain

Nicholas Bradley

ON BEING ARCHAIC

> *But there is no going back in time*
> —Al Purdy, "On Being Human"

Tuesdays and Thursdays
I meet my classes
and each time surmise
again that each student
is half as old as their teacher,
while they, I imagine,
watch him step cautiously
into the room, one foot
dangling in a private,
unimaginable
middle age beyond
even curiosity.

Each time we talk
about poems written
before any of us
was born, that some of us
love, and that none of us,
I worry, understands.

And I remember
my teachers, ancient
men and women
in their fifties and forties
(and sometimes younger)
who taught me the same
old poems, who must
have fathomed the rift
between us. And maybe

they disliked or feared
it as well, and maybe
they saw with clarity
how little I knew
and banished the thought
so we could continue
our game, throwing
from third to second to short
to first without the yips
getting in the way.

We size each other up
from across our field,
none of us able to say
just the right thing,
and now and then glance,
as the hour passes,
Tuesdays and Thursdays,
through the window
at metrical lines of rain

David Helwig

AT QUEEN'S PARK

We cross the park—a burly
victim of bad luck and not enough
cash asleep on the grass
among the strollers in the August sun,
and the murmuring green leaves say
that old trees grow tall.

We know what we're searching for,
make out the dark figure across the wide
green public space as the cars
motor round their circle and bronzed
bearded Edward the Seventh stands
sentry over his mother's park.

Al Purdy, Poet. I read the plaque,
study the monument, bigger, you'd say
than life size. But he always was. The head
turns far to one side on the long neck
listening for a distant sound or watching
some pretty girl passing in 1956.

I stand there as I planned to, wait
for some appropriate thought to shape itself
or maybe a remembered line or two, expect
a hyperbolic joke, to hear the sound
of a familiar voice—an unexpected phrase
from the other side of light.

I listen, wait for it, the tall man's
latest trick, what he might have to say
about being immortalized in a public park
among pissing dogs and shitting pigeons

and sleeping homeless men, and the late
last lostness of everything,

like the ghost mouth of Pushkin's stone guest
the metal lips to open with a whim
or jape by cosmic radio from Ameliasburgh,
whispering across the fields of eternity,
beyond the limits of silence the ventriloquist
offering his one last unlikely and phantasmal poem.

Susan Musgrave

THIRTY-TWO USES FOR AL PURDY'S ASHES

Smuggle them to Paris and fling them
into the Seine. PS He was wrong
when he wrote, "To Paris Never Again"

Put them in an egg-timer—that way
he can go on being useful, at least
for three minutes at a time
(pulverize him first, in a blender)

Like his no good '48 Pontiac
refusing to turn over in below zero weather,
let the wreckers haul his ashes away

Or stash them in the trunk of your car:
when you're stuck in deep snow sprinkle them
under your bald tires for traction

Mix them with twenty tons of concrete,
like Lawrence at Taos, erect
a permanent monument to his banned
poetry in Fenelon Falls

Shout "these ashes oughta be worth some beer!"
in the tavern at the Quinte Hotel, and wait
for a bottomless glass with yellow flowers in it
to appear

Mix one part ashes to three parts
homemade beer in a crock under the table,
stir with a broom, and consume
in excessive moderation

Fertilize the dwarf trees at the Arctic Circle
so that one day they might grow to be
as tall as he, always the first
to know when it was raining

Scatter them at Roblin's Mills
to shimmer among the pollen
or out over Roblin Lake
where the great *boing* they make
will arouse summer cottagers

Place them beside your bed where they can
watch you make love, vulgarly
and immensely, in the little time left

Declare them an aphrodisiac, more potent
than the gallbladder of a bear
with none of the side-effects of Viagra

Stitch them in the hem of your summer dress
where his weight will keep it
from flying up in the wind, exposing
everything: he would like that

Let them harden, the way the heart must harden
as the might lessens, then lob them
at the slimy, drivelling, snivelling,
palsied, pulseless lot of critics who ever uttered
a single derogatory phrase in anti-praise
of his poetry

Award them the Nobel Prize
for humility

Administer them as a dietary supplement
to existential Eskimo dogs with a preference

for violet toilet paper and violent
appetites for human excrement: dogs
that made him pray daily
for constipation in Pangnirtung

Bequeath them to Margaret Atwood,
casually inserted between the covers
of Wm Barrett's IRRATIONAL MAN

Lose them where the ghosts of his Cariboo
horses graze on, when you stop to buy oranges
from the corner grocer at 100 Mile House

Distribute them from a hang-glider
over the Galapagos Islands
where blue-footed boobies will shield him
from over-exposure to ultraviolet rays

Offer them as a tip to the shoeshine boys
on the Avenida Juarez, all twenty of them
who once shined his shoes for one peso
and 20 centavos—9 and a half cents—
years ago when 9 and a half cents
was worth twice that amount

Encapsulate them in the ruins of Quintana Roo
under the green eyes of quetzals, Tulum parrots,
and the blue, unappeasable sky—
that 600 years later they may still be warm

Declare them culturally modified property
and have them preserved for posterity
in the Museum of Modern Man, and, as
he would be the first to add, Modern Wife

As a last resort auction them off

to the highest bidder, the archives
at Queens or Cornell where
Auden's tarry lungs wheeze on
next to the decomposed kidneys of Dylan Thomas;
this will ensure Al's survival in Academia, also

But on no account cast his ashes to the wind:
they will blow back in your face as if to say
he is, in some form, poetic or other, here
to stay, with sestinas still to write
and articles to rewrite
for *The Imperial Oil Review*

No, give these mortal remains away
that they be used as a mojo to end the dirty
cleansing in Kosovo, taken as a cure
for depression in Namu, BC, for defeat
in the country north of Belleville, for poverty
hopping a boxcar west out of Winnipeg
all the way to Vancouver, for heroin addiction
in Vancouver; a cure for loneliness
in North Saanich, for love in Oaxaca,
courtship in Cuernavaca, adultery
in Ameliasburgh, the one sure cure
for extremely deep hopelessness
in the Eternal City, for death, everywhere,
pressed in a letter sent whispering to you

Laurence Hutchman

AL PURDY'S PLACE

I

I turn onto the road leading to Ameliasburgh.
Nearly twenty years since
I visited this place where
you wandered under the large beams,
through the old grist mill,
in searching for dusty motes of sunlight
until you stared into the face of Owen Roblin.

The '73 Ford is gone,
your tall lanky figure does not stride to meet me again.
The waters of Roblin Lake are rough.
Around broken boards I step
to see blue wooden chairs weathered on the deck;
Eurithe, Michael Ondaatje and Margaret Laurence
would have drunk beer here late into the summer's night.

The old cabin you built as a study is locked.
In the box by the door I see a lamp
that would have shone light
on your hiccoughing typewriter, on the poems
that spoke of Fidel on Revolutionary Square,
of Gus and you before the Kremlin,
searching for the ghost of Helen in the dusty city of Troy,
recounting the tough, angry Tarahumara women in Mexico,
the scenes evoking the ghosts of Machu Picchu and your friend Earl.

You sat in that study until it became the freight car:
across the prairies into the sudden mountains,
until the dust of the land entered you in those voices,
speaking now through your poems.

You were working on *Reaching for the Beaufort Sea,*
talking about time,
how we continually mourn the past,
how we live on a thin edge,
a slice of time that exists only in the present
before it becomes the past.

II

I remember the letter from Ameliasburgh
that invited me to send you poems.
I still hear your distinct voice,
with its currents of wit and humour,
a gusto, a buildup and release.
I remember the time in Montreal at El Gitano
after so much sangria
when we argued poetry late into the night.

Through the rough gravel of Purdy Lane,
I drive to the cemetery alongside the river.
There, in the wet grass is the black shiny tome
with the words, "The Voice of the Land."
Someone has left a note
and stuck a ballpoint pen in the earth.

Lorna Crozier

A CAT NAMED PURDY

If Al comes back
it will be as something gaunt and big—
a tree perhaps, like Thompson's pine
he tore from a calendar and taped
on the bathroom wall. The last thing
I'd expect is a cat. Unlike Eliot

he didn't like them. Our last cat
we'd called Nowlan. When I told Al
we'd name our new one Purdy, he shouted,
waved his arms and almost threw me out
though we'd been having a grand time
reciting from memory Leda and the Swan
line by line to one another, our voices
loud above the beating of the wings.

His favourite in-law, Eurithe's sister Norma,
for years has rescued cats. She finds them
in the wild, brings them home and gentles them
until they're tame enough to give away. Maybe
she'll find him wandering beyond the world
of doors and windows, beyond the glow
from someone's reading lamp,

and he'll be coaxed inside, wet and matted,
eyes a little mad, Norma, whom,
when he was alive he also loved,
offering a bowl of milk to calm him,
her flannel shirt to keep him warm.

To take this story further and why not,
Eurithe, now that she's alone, will be persuaded

to accept a scruffy stray—long-limbed,
ungainly for a cat. With quintessential Purdy
I-don't-give-a-damn paired with a cat's
he'll leap into her lap that's not
welcomed one in years, he'll sigh and purr.

And with his paws, big as his hands
when he was a boy but now not clumsy
or afraid, he'll retract
his claws and knead the softness of that
oh, familiar flesh.

ELEGIES

Doug Paisley

LAST NIGHT

The saddest thing I guess
Was I've grown used to being here
More familiar than I'd imagined
What's left is the everyday
The faces are all on photographs
The voices are on cassettes
I can visit them over and over
Like we think we'd like to do
You're over on the other side of the water
No longer fearful of the dark, I hope
These are the same birds but they wouldn't know you
They navigate through blinking towers
And narrowing corridors
I wouldn't bother telling you a damn thing about this world
Selfish isn't it?
No one waited like you did
No one could enjoy it when it came like you could
Now you're waiting for everything to hurry up and end
One night at a time

Doug Beardsley

BREAKOUT

At 100 Mile House I try to make sense
of the place 40 years after the fact
of your poem & the book that made
the Purdy name a household word

& this broken-down town, empty of horses
Cariboo or otherwise & no people either—
        if you discount grinning Secwepemc kids
        from Canim Lake or bored housewives
        feeling their first biodynamic massage
        in spas sheltered beneath toy mountains
without substance, without weight. No more

horses here, historical, ancient or
anywhichway only *the ghosts of horses*
& you BIG AL, tall in the saddle beyond all measure
gripping the reins ham-fisted
saddle-bags chocked full of a lifetime
of hands-on experience, readings & poems
stirrups digging in for the last long ride.

Julie McNeill

TRAINS, BEER & BRONZE
the voice of the land

Years after train cars
took your young man's voice
and roughened it
took your impressionable ears
and pounded into them
the pulse of Canada
       you brewed people's poetry
       in the A-frame's simplicity
       and shared it

After the published books
you ambled into the lecture hall
shirtsleeves rolled up
and gave thirsty students
tales for All the Annettes,
The Cariboo Horses...
       and carried the hangers-on
       to the windy patios
       of rooftop bars

Today I hear your voice
in the wind blowing across Queen's Park
your loose shirt draped in light snow
the pocket pen & notebook cold
but your pages filled
with rich warm poems
       while other poets sit in the A-frame
       wondering where you've gone
       leaving wet rings under beer glasses

Patrick Lane

FOR AL PURDY

It wasn't the brawling man who wrote of *dangerous women with whiskey-coloured eyes*, it was the other man I knew in '62, the awkward one you hid inside the Contact book, the one who spoke of lines that never end. That's what I heard first and that's the man I knew. It was the uneasiness you had with the myth you'd made of yourself. You were a mama's boy and spoiled like only-children are. Even your ride on the freight train back in the thirties wasn't a real struggle, was more adventure than endurance. Survival had nothing to do with it, though later you'd learn, picking through Air Force garbage with Eurithe to keep food on the table. Three days in Vancouver and you couldn't wait to hop a freight back to Ontario, homesick, a little scared. Suffering was never your strong point. It took Eurithe to help you with that. But I remember '66, the night we left the Cecil to visit Newlove on Yew Street and giddy with drink I threw a full bottle of beer at the sky. You stopped dead and waited till the bottle fell and smashed. *Only throw empty bottles at the moon*, you said, shaking your head at the waste of a drink. It's a metaphor I've lived with in this life, that moon. Or the time we stole books at the McStew Launch in '73. You told me to stop taking the poetry. *Take the picture books*, you said. *No one will give you money for a poem.* Jack McClelland was railing at us and Newlove was dancing drunk on a table while Farley glowered in a corner because he wasn't the centre of attention. Clarkson was prissy and Layton was trying once again to get laid. God knows where Acorn was. All names now, men and women either dead or getting closer. And you? I could talk with you about the attributes of *Rubus spectabilis* and Etruscan tombs. We could go from there to a discussion about the relative venom of *Laticauda colubrina*. You liked the leaps and made a poetry from space. You went from the yellow-lipped sea krait to the eyes of Eurithe and found love at the end of your complaint. I think love was at the heart of all you did, the only loss you knew. Not knowing what you should learn, you learned everything. An autodidact (I loved that word when I was young, it gave my ignorance a name) you put in everything you could, your mind moving like your body, a poem too big to fit into the world. Sitting at the kitchen table three months before your death you told me you'd never had a friend. *Are you my friend?*

you asked. I'll never forget your eyes. There were never any cheap tricks in your art. It's the one thing you taught me. *Don't tell it slant*, you might've said. Your poems were Möbius strips. Following your mind was like my wandering in South America years ago. I knew there was no end, it was the going I had to learn, the nowhere we all get to. I split the word these days. Right now I'm here. You liked the story of me almost dying from a centipede sting in the jungle east of Ecuador, the little brown woman who nursed me back to life as she fed me soup made from boiled *cuy*. Like most men you liked stories. All your confessions were metaphors, those tired horses in the dust at Hundred Mile the measure. Or the time you made coffee in the frying pan in Toronto for Lorna and me, the bubbles of bacon grease just something to add body to the day. With you I could almost make it through. I fixed your deathbed, the second-hand you and Eurithe bought at a garage sale. You stood in a reel while I hammered it together. Three days later you were gone. I could say I still have words but none of them add up to you. Whispers mostly in the racket. Poems go round and round, this one too, never quite getting there, but I still live, and your *ivory thought* is all that keeps me warm some nights, still writing, still alive. It's a cheap out, Al, but where else to go but back to you grabbing picture books, telling me once again that poems don't sell. They never did.

Autumn Richardson

THE ORACLE

Scars, glacial drift, bog-
cotton, dwarf willow

nameless lakes—cold has stripped
all colour from their waves

there is no compassion here, except
that which I carry for small things

yet still I throw lines into water to lure
what may feed me, bones onto flames
to see the art that carbon makes

what I see there:

this day is a momentary haven;
an interval between longer notes

pines are shifting into crows; the wolf
is a deer's viscera; each is becoming
another's vision, another's gait

and so I drink the trees

soon my salts will feed the next
short sharp life.

Susan Musgrave

AL PURDY TOOK A BUS TO THE TOWN WHERE HERODOTUS WAS BORN

"The town we visited," Al says, "remember
the town—we caught a bus there."
Eurithe can't remember the name of the place,
either, but she recalls a wake-up call
and a foreign voice saying "Your cold breakfast
is coming up." The last time I made Al
a birthday cake it fell, but Al was gracious
enough to say *thank you for your largesse.*

There are vast areas of my ————
that are missing, for instance the name
of the restaurant in Dublin where each dish
was an approximation of its ideal,
or the Christian names of my daughter's
school bus drivers I said I'd never forget:
Mrs. Blood, Mr. Wolf, and Miss Hood.
I wanted to write a Young Adult book
about "the late bus," the one the bad kids
always took, but I didn't want my obituary
ending up in the Entertainment Section
of the newspaper where I once found a prognosis
of Elizabeth Taylor's tumour. I don't want
to be anybody's Smile of the Day
which is why I'm glad I didn't shoot myself
cleaning Henry White's house on Haida Gwaii
last summer—my death would have made
the *National Enquirer* along with Wife Used
Cheating Hubby's Toothbrush to Clean the Commode.
In Henry White's house I sucked up a .22 bullet,
heard a bang, saw sparks, and the next thing
I remember I was seeing headlines: Woman Shoots Self

in Head with Vacuum Cleaner. The photograph
of my sad brain looks like a honeydew melon
soaked in V8 Juice all night after being run over
by a train the time I went pub-hopping in Oxford
and landed in a punk bar eating drugged cookies
which I worried about later when I started
hallucinating because I was pregnant
with Charlotte and didn't want her to be born
in the corridor of British Rail while I peaked
on Peek Freans Digestive Biscuits. Mary Oliver
says poems are ropes let down to the lost, I wish
someone would keep that in mind when they ever
find me. A critic in the *Globe* asks why
poets are always *losing* things, especially
people, why can't they *find* something
instead, and I believe he deserves an answer.

"The town where they lost your suitcase," Al says,
"remember the town—we caught a bus there."
Eurithe can't remember if her luggage showed up
but she does recall a wake-up call, a foreign
voice saying, "Your hour has come," and the line
going dead. You cherish people
then they are gone: what more can be said
about the ones I'd rather be with,
the ones I love best.

I thank them for their largesse.

Susan Musgrave

EACH LIFE IS A LANGUAGE NO ONE KNOWS

It went well. That's what the man who helped take
my friend's life said after my friend drank a last glass
of Chilean wine laced with date rape drug
and then allowed his helper to place an Exit Bag
from a box marked Party Balloon Kits
on my friend's head, and pump him full of helium. *It went
well.* That's what the man said to my friend's wife
who waited in the living room, in her dressing gown
dwelling deeply in her own thoughts and feelings.

Whose thoughts and feelings—apart from her own—
might she have dwelt upon? The man said the inflated
helium bag rose above my friend's head like a chef's hat
before being pulled down over his face. I like to think
my friend drifted up and away into that unknown country
he had written about, but death that day
was the sound of one cold hand clapping as I made my way
back down my friend's driveway, which looked as if
it had been paved recently with crushed bones. *It went
well.* A person spends his life saying goodbye
to other people. How does he say goodbye to himself?

Tom Wayman

IN MEMORY OF A.W. PURDY

(d. Apr. 2000)

Death came for him in the spring:
a dark crocus.
For even winter, that emblem of
age and aridity,
sickens and dies
and by that act nurtures
a different season. The snow, the crocuses
appear and vanish repeatedly:
the spinning biosphere they help form
is bound in turn to a rotating planet
—on which Al Purdy lived once
and just once.

Sid Marty phoned
from his ranch up Willow Valley Road
in the Alberta foothills
to let me know.
"*All* the fathers are dying," I responded
—my own father, exhausted to the core by a hospital's
intrusive and agonizing procedures
to restore one collapsed bodily system after another,
had convinced his doctors the previous May to grant
the peace of the hospice ward
in which he could sleep his solitary way out of the world.
"This point in our lives," I told Marty,
"must have happened to our fathers, also."

"We've been able to paddle around,"
Marty mused, "in the shallows
as long as they were beyond us out in the open ocean.

Now we have to voyage
where they went, onto deep water."

I remembered a poem by Earle Birney,
Purdy's old colleague, now lost as he under the long swells
of the expanse with no further shore: *That sea
is hight Time,*
Birney wrote, adopting an archaic tongue,
we drift to map's end.

II

Purdy shambled across the earth, a big man
whose hands en route pushed at a taxi meter, at
pens, at newly manufactured mattresses,
used books, typewriters, the edges of lecterns,
case after case of beer.
As he travelled, he delighted in
the contours of the landscape,
its swales and bluffs, ridges and
hollows. He marvelled, too,
at much he discovered among this geology:
electrical switchyards, grainfields, magistrate's courtrooms
and the men and women who inhabit each region or district,
with their dogs, flower beds, rusted-out cars.

On everything Purdy loved most
he bestowed
the name of his country.
Yet he was wrong.
In the forest that straddles the border here, the firs
on each side do not clutch
differing small flags in their twigs.
The Great Divide, as mapmakers understand,

occurs along another line.
Still, Purdy did not know what else to do
with his huge affection for all he encountered.
He gazed at what pleased him
with the proprietary eyes
of pure joy. He called it *Canada*, but
it was Purdy.

III

Now the poet lives in his words, which
as Purdy himself would note,
is a damn strange constricted airless waterless
place to live
—no rhubarb pies or Molson's Ale,
no girls in their flirty summer tops.

And any language can die, or change shape
until only pedants and their victims
are able to drudge through it:
maybe one in ten thousand of these
feels the neuron's spark of wit in a phrase
or description regarded as ironic or humorous by a former time.

Yet those weakest of constructs—words, poems—
have endured centuries
so far, which given the track record of
most things humans create and believe in
isn't shabby at all. So perhaps some of Purdy's words
will stumble a little tipsily into the future

viewing wonders—and possibly horrors—he now
won't be able to see for himself.
His gift to me

was his rambling: his itinerant lines and
peripatetic stanzas—apparently relaxed, inquisitive, opinionated,
exactly like someone talking:

a conversation with the reader so cunningly shaped
that the choice of structure or other artistic details
is not the point of the piece, any more than a news story
reveals its architecture. His boozy self-confidence
took poetry to a place nobody else had been.
Who cares? you say. I care,

and maybe the eons will. If not, his life and achievements
were no less futile than those of the rest of us.
I drive back from town on an asphalt road
dry in the middle of the lanes now that the rain has passed.
Over my truck's speakers
I hear a guitar chord struck,

then a second one, and a human voice
begins to chant a story,
singing me home.
Purdy wasn't a singer, even if a fan or reviewer
occasionally waxed rhetorical.
But when he depressed a key

and the shaft lifted and fell toward the paper,
that passage of metal through air vibrated like
two people who argue in bed or
in a bar, a coyote taunting the Valley dogs,
the raucous blast of a diesel train engine
that approaches a crossing, a class of grade twos

squawking their version of anybody's national anthem,
a bellow from a steer in Kooznetsoff's field
along the Lower Road, wind

swooping over tundra.
And since Al Purdy was at ease
with the currents and rollers of Time, I'll add

that the sound was whatever noise dinosaurs uttered
in an amorous mood, the *skritch-skritch* of a quill pen,
a choir in full flight during a requiem mass
(okay, maybe he did sing a little),
a black crocus breaking through soil
into the light of day.

John Watson

VARIATIONS

> *It's like coming out of a dark room*
> *to find yourself*
> *under the wheat blaze*
> *of a Saskatchewan sky*
> —Al Purdy

A sky of wheat
Saskatchewan blue

Stepping into the light:
Saskatchewan wheat sky

To find yourself
find a Saskatchewan sky

In 2000 Al Purdy
comes out of a dark room
into the wheat blaze
of a Saskatchewan sky

Phil Hall

from AN OAK HUNCH: ESSAY ON PURDY

IN THESE PROVINCIAL JERK-WATERS
turnpiked by eagles

  his carbon & foolscap
local Legion
            o wouldst thee lyrics

  (stumbling in dark plowed-under cornfields

widening & falling—in arrogance with flaws
  dismissively monumentous)

glance against the sublime!

  he discovers sublime limestone
where all of the old surveys wallow white

  HIS COCKY DEFIANCE DROPS AWAY
increasingly awe is its own music

  a surety of doubt-tone visits
after years of homemade laments & elegies

  his Opeongo eyes take in & translate
a petrified flaming tongue's filibuster

when are *you coming down again*

how are you getting on with the two new ones

THE TRAILS HE CHOPPED NORTH FOR OUR COLONIES
of inattention (Romanticism as History's axe)

stop behind us now—hacked markers—a pile of stanchions & cables

staggered images—almost *mayday*—perhaps caught

NOW EVERY JACK LIAR & THIEF
reflected in the black granite

gravestone of *the voice of the land*
reads "book" as "voice's tomb"

& carries home some keepsake
(a stone or cement chicken)

the giant & I went way back
he gave me this before he died

but thrown stones are talking
stolen cement chickens are talking

the land's voice sacred noise
thunder & lightning unlike us

SHOCKED AWAKE
by a speck of red on a white A

woodpecker
on the slushy tin roof of this unfinished A-frame

wrong with gusto
now both of us hammering away   *damn radio plays*

blood untribalized—territories amplified
art a quirk-of-patience lingo

                         that lifts the tongue of the sky

  there is always a better thunder
pending than gatling   *but gatling pays*

PITY WHAT IS LEFT OF US & OUR COUNTRY
as we dismantle & burn for cheap warmth

  the guy-tropes he brought forward on his back
to get us here & past here

STOP IN A DARK FIELD

his white shirt—jacklit—glows
  tails out among stones

a white shirt & a hockey stick
  whacking rocks into the trees

then stopping to listen

THE FALL WIND RUSHING THROUGH THE DRY CORN
in all of the cornfields for miles around here

  the paper applause of an ancient voice
that has just come around with some news

  the roll-your-own salvos of the wind in the corn

a standing ovation surrounding each farmhouse

  sh bravura sh

BIOGRAPHIES
AND
STATEMENTS

Milton Acorn (1923–86) was a friend of Purdy's; their sometimes fractious relationship is captured in Purdy's poem "House Guest." Three of Acorn's poetry collections were edited by Purdy, however. Acorn was a fervent Canadian nationalist; two books of his poems were published by the now-defunct Canadian Liberation Movement. He "was a Communist and a traditional Conservative," James Deahl writes. "Not at different times; at the same time." In 1970 a group of fellow poets presented a medal to Acorn, dubbing him "the People's Poet." He won the 1975 Governor General's Literary Award for poetry.

Solveig Adair has lived in many places, but her body, like her writing, is drawn inexorably back to the small towns of the North. Solveig has been published in a number of journals and anthologies including, most recently, *Dreamworks, filling Station* and *Snow Feathers*.

As someone growing up in a small northern town, there were few voices that spoke in the clear beautiful unforgiving language that I saw reflected in the world around me. As a young teenager, I found a worn copy of *Wild Grape Wine* and a lifelong love affair was born. Al Purdy gave voice to the people I met and knew. He allowed them to survive long after the communities they established faded back into poverty and obscurity. As for me, what he gave me is perhaps best said by Al Purdy himself. The pictures painted by his poems are etched within me and, as in the closing lines of "The Last Picture in the World," it occurs to me "that if I were to die at this moment / that picture would accompany me / wherever I am going / for part of the way."

James Arthur grew up in Toronto. His first book, *Charms Against Lightning*, was published by Copper Canyon Press. His work also has appeared in *The New Yorker*, *The New York Review of Books*, *The London Review of Books*, *Poetry*, *Brick* and *The New Republic*. Arthur teaches at Johns Hopkins University.

During the summer of 2017, I spent two months in residence at the Purdy A-frame in Ameliasburgh, writing. I never met Purdy when he was alive, and never heard him read except on tape—but his poems were part of my education, and I deeply admire his decision to organize his life around poetry, without compromise, and without much encouragement either, at least during those early years.

I hope that my poem explains itself. I wanted to pay tribute to Al Purdy, and also capture the experience of living in another writer's house, surrounded by his things, trying to understand one's own life by understanding someone else's.

Something I wanted to work into the poem and couldn't was the blue heron that came every few days to wade in the shallows of Roblin Lake. It couldn't possibly have been the same heron that Purdy cast as a harbinger of death, twenty years earlier, in his late poem, "The Last Picture in the World" ("A hunched grey shape / framed by leaves / with lake water behind / standing on our / little point of land / like a small monk")—and yet it was hard to see the bird any other way.

Ken Babstock is a poet, editor and teacher. His collection *Airstream Land Yacht* (House of Anansi, 2006) was a finalist for the Governor General's Literary Award. His collection *Methodist Hatchet* (House of Anansi, 2011) won the Griffin Poetry Prize.

Doug Beardsley was born and raised in Montreal. After Expo 67 he spent a year in Connecticut, followed by three years in England and two in France. He returned to Canada in 1974, settling on the West Coast in Victoria.

In the fall of 1974, Al came to read at the University of Victoria. I was immediately aware that this giant of a man was a giant poet. Our friendship began when we discovered we were fellow sufferers and devoted fans of the Toronto Maple Leafs. Weekly lunches and intense conversations about poets and poetry developed into two book collaborations and the idea for a third.

Gregory Betts is the author of seven books of poetry, editor of five books of experimental Canadian writing, and author of *Avant-Garde Canadian Literature: The Early Manifestation*. He is the Artistic Director of the Festival of Readers, the Curator of the bpNichol.ca Digital Archive, and a professor at Brock University.

The first time I imagined a living poetry was in Kingston, Ontario, down deep on Princess Street halfway toward the water. Coming out of the repertory cinema, after seeing *Bleu* (the first, and best, of Krzysztof Kieślowski's trilogy), we saw there was a light snow falling, but we were excited by the movie and walked to talk until we came across a crowd spilling out of the Sleepless Goat café. Curious, and drunk with the spirit of the night, we pushed our way in to find a long, gaunt man holding forth. Every word moved in a charmed air from him out to every ear around the room. In the film, we'd just seen Juliette Binoche fall in ecstasy at a printed line of music. I'd never seen a poet in their natural element before. Beside him was Eurithe, with whom we spoke after the reading had ended. I asked her who the poet was, and she said without smiling, "Oh, that's just Al." People jostled us from behind for blocking the book table. I felt like a turnstile at the gates of a secret garden. I'm not sure what it was about the event, but two things happened immediately after the reading: I scrambled to assemble a small chapbook of my own writing (but gave it to no one), and I bought a book of poetry (*Poems for All the Annettes*, recommended by Prof. Ware) for the first time of my own accord.

Earle Birney (1904–95) was arguably the pre-eminent Canadian modernist poet, twice winner of the Governor General's Literary Award for his poems. He was "a friend, a model and a mentor" to Purdy, in the words of Birney's biographer, Elspeth Cameron. "I look at Birney's poem 'Bushed' as an example of somewhere near the way I'd like to write," Purdy said. "Behind that poem is a whole universe of meaning waiting for the reader." In 2014 Harbour published the 1947–87 letters between Birney and Purdy, *We Go Far Back in Time*, edited by Nicholas Bradley. "As I grow old," Purdy wrote, "I think of myself as a slightly older Birney (discontent, cantankerous…and damn well other points of similarity, too)."

George Bowering is a Vancouver poet who has often written about Al Purdy and his work. He first stayed overnight in the A-frame in the sixties, and did so again in the twenty-first century. He is fortunate enough to be married to Jean Baird, who started the movement to save the A-frame. His most recent book of poetry is *Some End*, his half of a flip book shared with George Stanley and published by New Star Books.

Nicholas Bradley lives in Victoria, BC. He is the author of *Rain Shadow* (University of Alberta Press, 2018), a collection of poems.

> I never met Al Purdy, though I heard him read once when I was a student. The poetry was lost on me then, and I was far too shy to introduce myself to the poet. Now, as a teacher of Canadian literature, I regret the missed opportunity whenever I read Purdy's poems in the classroom, my imitation of his voice reminding me that I heard the real thing only for a half-hour that I can scarcely recall. In time, his poems showed me something of what it means to be here, and I am grateful to the good teachers who helped me listen to that unmistakable voice on the page.

Kate Braid has written, co-written or co-edited fourteen books and chapbooks of non-fiction and prize-winning poetry. For fifteen years she worked in construction though she now builds entirely in words. See www.katebraid.com.

> Especially when I became involved in construction, Purdy's down-to-earthness and rough humour (just like construction guy-humour) were a continual affirmation that I was on the right track, that it was okay to write about work, to say it plainly, to aim to communicate with so-called "ordinary" people. Thank you Al Purdy, indeed!

Brian Brett, former chair of The Writers' Union of Canada and a journalist for four decades, is best known as a poet, memoir writer, and fictionist. He is the author of thirteen books and was the 2016 recipient of the Writers' Trust Matt Cohen Award for Lifetime Achievement.

Kat Cameron is the author of two collections of poetry: *Strange Labyrinth* (Oolichan Books, 2015) and *Lightning over Wyoming* (Oolichan Books, 2018). Her poetry, fiction and book reviews have appeared in over fifty journals and anthologies. She teaches English literature and writing at Concordia University of Edmonton.

Until the summer of 2017, when I took a writing workshop with Steven Heighton, I wasn't very familiar with Purdy's poetry. I had read "Trees at the Arctic Circle" and loved some of the lines, especially the description of the trees whose "seed pods glow / like delicate grey earrings." Heighton's enthusiasm for Purdy's poetry inspired me to read Rosemary Sullivan's essay "Purdy's Dark Cowboy" in *Memory-Making,* and I decided to teach "Lament for the Dorsets" in a first-year English class. After explaining the history of the Dorset people and showing an image of a two-inch swan carving, I had the students write a paragraph analyzing Purdy's use of history in the poem. Some answers depressed me; some astounded me. One student thought that the poem was about actual giants. But another recognized that Purdy is "piecing together stories" from Dorset artifacts. This is the work of poets: piecing together stories. Purdy's poem reimagines the past, creating what Sullivan calls a magic "of memory and place." Like Purdy and the Dorset carver he imagines, I write from "the places in [my] mind / where pictures are."

Bruce Cockburn is a distinguished Canadian singer-songwriter. He has received thirteen Juno Awards, is an officer of the Order of Canada and a winner of the Governor General's Performing Arts Award for Lifetime Artistic Achievement. His autobiography, *Rumours of Glory*, was published in 2014.

I went out and got Purdy's collected works, which is an incredible book. Then I had this vision of a homeless guy who is obsessed with Purdy's poetry, and he's ranting it on the street. The song is written in the voice of that character. The chorus goes, "I'll give you three Al Purdys for a twenty dollar bill." Here's this grey-haired dude, coattails flapping in the wind, being mistaken for the sort of addled ranters you run into on the street—except he's not really ranting, he's reciting Al Purdy. The spoken word parts of the track are excerpts from Purdy's poems. After that, once the ice was broken, the songs just started coming.

Lorna Crozier's latest book is *What the Soul Doesn't Want*, published in 2017 and nominated for the Governor General's Award. In 2015 two books came out: *The Wrong Cat*, which received her third Pat Lowther Award, and *The Wild in You*, a collaboration with photographer Ian McAllister. She's an Officer of the Order of Canada, the recipient of the Governor General's Award, the George Woodcock Lifetime Achievement Award, BC's Lieutenant Governor's Award for Literary Excellence, and five honorary doctorates, most recently from McGill and Simon Fraser. Born in Saskatchewan, she lives on Vancouver Island.

Robert Currie is the author of seven books of poetry and four works of fiction. He served as Saskatchewan's third Poet Laureate and received the 2009 Saskatchewan Lieutenant Governor's Award for Lifetime Achievement in the Arts. His most recent book is *The Days Run Away* (Coteau, 2015).

Al Purdy was the first poet I'd ever seen. There he was in 1965, at the University of Saskatchewan, live, unlike most of the poets we took in class. His poems, too, were full of life, original and gripping, nothing stuffy about this man or his work. Hearing him read made me want to read more of his poems, and though I was too shy to approach him then, I later bought *The Cariboo Horses*. Reading that collection was exciting; it enhanced a compulsion I was already feeling to write poems of my own. In those early years I was lucky to be inspired by Al Purdy.

Some years later I applied for membership in the League of Canadian Poets and asked for a recommendation from Ron Everson, whom I'd published in *Salt*, a little magazine that I was grinding out in the seventies on a borrowed Gestetner. Ron wrote that he'd be happy to recommend me, and so would Al, who was there for a visit. Al who, I wondered. No, it couldn't possibly be, but when I looked at the letter there was the signature of Al Purdy. What could be better than that?

Rodney DeCroo is a poet, singer-songwriter and actor. He grew up in a small coal town in western Pennsylvania, USA, but has lived in Vancouver for many years. He has published two collections of poetry with Nightwood Editions. He has released eight albums through Northern Electric Records and his current label, Tonic Records. DeCroo also wrote a one-man show, *Stupid Boy in an Ugly Town*, that has toured throughout Canada and was featured at the Vancouver International Writers Festival.

Sadiqa de Meijer was born in Amsterdam, and moved to Canada as a child. Her poetry, short stories and essays have appeared in many journals and anthologies, and in 2012 she won the CBC Poetry Prize. Her first collection, *Leaving Howe Island* (Oolichan Books, 2014), was a finalist for the Governor General's Award.

I spent a July at the A-frame, and I will always be grateful for how seamless life could feel there; I was writing in a space with an animate past, I was making a living, my child was having glorious days at the beach. But what I need to write about here is another aspect of my stay. I grappled with the books on the A-frame shelves; there were many white, anthropological perspectives on Indigenous and tribal cultures, the sort of studies that are almost zoological in tone. At the same time, when I walked the county roads, I was often struck by how the landscape resembled parts of the Netherlands, where I grew up. As an immigrant writer of mixed race, I found the place was in conversation with several parts of me. Someone in my background could have written the books in question, and someone else could have been their subject. Someone would have known how to farm the sandy ground. The poem "Ancestor vs. Ancestor" is an A-frame poem because the voice is aligned with those who wrote the books, or at least with their antecedents. In this chance to speak again, they seem to both explain and disown their actions.

Magie Dominic, Newfoundland writer and artist, lives in New York. She is the author of the memoirs *The Queen of Peace Room* and *Street Angel*. Her writing has been published in multiple periodicals. Her art has been exhibited at the United Nations and in several cities, including Toronto and New York.

Al Purdy's unique ability to give a personality, a human face, to weather, trees and the elements, to all aspects of the environment and geography, is both an inspiration to me as a writer, and a source of great joy to me as a reader.

The geographical location for Purdy's "Trees at the Arctic Circle," and his voice in the poem, inspired me to write "Standing on a Newfoundland Cliff."

The geographical settings for both poems address nature, geography and survival and adaptation to unique environments.

To me, Purdy's poem, "Trees at the Arctic Circle," addresses "the symbolic elements of the self in nature and in the environment. This is an aspect I have approached in my writing and continue to approach.

The trees in "Trees at the Arctic Circle" are diametrically opposite to the tuckamore trees in "Standing on a Newfoundland Cliff" but both species of trees, both personalities, are unquestionable survivors.

Dymphny Dronyk works as a mediator for Alberta Justice and is a translator, editor and writing coach. Her collection *Contrary Infatuations* (Frontenac House, 2007) was shortlisted for the Pat Lowther Award and the Stephan G. Stephansson Award for Poetry. She is the publisher of several bestselling anthologies at House of Blue Skies.

I discovered Al's poetry as a young teen, living in a cabin off the grid in the Kootenays. There was something so earthy, and evocative, and playful about his work that I imagined that he would understand my quirky, marginalized existence. I banged out poems on a crooked old typewriter, where every lowercase *e* was a half line above the other letters, and dreamed that one day I too would be a poet. His poems made me believe that I could write about my life, as it was, and that was a gift like no other.

Candace Fertile teaches at Camosun College in Victoria, BC.

Purdy's poetry runs the gamut of emotions, just as his language includes everything from the vulgar to the erudite. In particular I love his ability to be funny and serious, often in the same poem as he does in "At the Quinte Hotel."

Katherine L. Gordon is a rural Ontario poet, publisher, judge, editor and reviewer, working to promote the voices of Canadian poets around the world. She has many books, chapbooks, anthologies and collaborations with fine contemporaries whose work inspires her. Her poems have received awards and been translated internationally. Latest book: *Piping at the End of Days* (Valley Press, 2017).

Richard M. Grove, otherwise known to friends as Tai, lives in Presqu'ile Provincial Park, Ontario, where he and his wife run a B&B, and where he also runs Hidden Brook Press. He is a poet, prose writer, publisher, photographer, painter, president. His many titles of poetry, prose and memoir can be found on Amazon.

Like many, I corresponded with Al Purdy by letter. I once mailed him one of my poems where I gave him credit for three lines from one of his poems that I had incorporated into my poem. His reply letter to me was humorous, as he often was: "Nice poem, at least it has three good lines." He and I laughed about this when I reminded him over a coffee in Toronto. The first time that I met him was at a reading where I presented a stack of books for him to sign for me. As I presented the stack of books I said, "This stack is proof that I am a big fan." His reply was, "There are a few titles missing from that stack."

I have always been impressed with Al Purdy's poems, so much so that I, as president of the Canada Cuba Literary Alliance, nominated him posthumously as the Canadian Ambassador for the CCLA. This idea was endorsed by his wife, Eurithe. The CCLA is proud to include one of his poems in every issue of *The Ambassador*.

Phil Hall's most recent books are *Conjugation* (BookThug, 2016), *Guthrie Clothing: The Poetry of Phil Hall—A Selected Collage* (Wilfrid Laurier University Press, 2015) and—with Erin Moure—*The Interrupted* (Beautiful Outlaw Press, 2017). He has won the Governor General's Award (2011) and Ontario's Trillium Award (2012). He has twice been nominated for the Griffin Poetry Prize. He is the director of the Page Lectures at Queen's University.

Rolf Harvey has a book of New and Selected due to be published in the latter half of 2019. "But I don't feel enthusiastic or even grateful now that I am seventy," he said. "I do feel good that my life's works, including years of work as a film designer, are somehow being recognized by a university's archives."

There are so many stories and times I had living down there in Ameliasburgh. In fact, I spent so much time down there when I was a bum, a broken man, and they gave me family. I used to take the train down and stay at Eurithe's mother's house to eat a butter tart or two (she used to make them for me when she heard I was getting off the train and walking over to her house). I'd sit there with tea and butter tarts waiting for Eurithe or Al to come to pick me up and travel out to the A-frame.

Anyway, I have stories and memories still from how she and he took care of me when I was a broken man. I lived down there off and on for years and so I got to know him and her much better, I think, than graduate students.

Steven Heighton received the 2016 Governor General's Award for poetry for *The Waking Comes Late* (Anansi). He was also a finalist in 1995 for *The Ecstasy of Skeptics* (Anansi). His poetry and stories have received five National Magazine Awards and have appeared in *London Review of Books, Poetry* (Chicago), *Tin House, Brick, Zoetrope, Best American Poetry, The Walrus, Best English Stories,* TLR and five editions of *Best Canadian Poetry.* He has also published novels, short story collections and two books of essays, and he reviews fiction for *The New York Times Book Review.*

David Helwig and Al Purdy first met in Kingston, Ontario, one summer afternoon in 1968. Over the next thirty years they both wrote and published a lot of poetry and prose, and they visited frequently. They last met at the Purdy house in Ameliasburgh shortly before Al and Eurithe made their final trip west.

Cornelia Hoogland's seventh book, *Trailer Park Elegy* (Harbour, 2017), is an elegiac long poem. *Woods Wolf Girl* was a finalist for the 2012 ReLit Award for Poetry. *Sea Level* was shortlisted for the 2012 CBC Nonfiction Prize, and *Tourists Stroll a Victoria Waterway* was shortlisted for the 2017 CBC Poetry Prize. www.corneliahoogland.com.

I never met Al Purdy, but feel I know something of the man and poet through his many books of poetry, his correspondence with Margaret Laurence—a book I treasure—as well as Paul Vermeersch's *The Al Purdy A-Frame Anthology* (Harbour, 2009). I came to my own poetry late, and missed making friendships with my poetry foremothers and forefathers. To remedy this as best I can, I both study and write poems about the older poets in my literary family. I feel I meet Al through Roblin Lake on which he lived much of his life, and in a handful of his poems, such as "Prince Edward County" where he writes: "Animals having no human speech / have not provided names / but named it with their bodies / and the long-ago pine forests / named it with their bodies / and the masts of sailing ships / around the century's turn / named it to the sea / and a bird one springtime / named it bobolink bobolink." This stanza looks outward, beyond Al Purdy and human immediacy, to the larger world. I picture him gazing aimlessly over the lake, just sitting there, looking. If it wasn't Al's poem I'd be tempted to say it's spiritual, so great its reach.

Wednesday Hudson lives in Calgary, sometimes Vancouver, and works as a realtor in both, a tale of two cities fraught with pro-pipeline and anti-pipeline energetics. Her mother always said things happen in threes so she has three boys and three dogs. She remains an untreated Purdy fanatic and confirmed student of Life.

I had only read a few of Al's poems before writing "For Eurithe." I wrote it in about ten minutes sitting on my fireplace ledge. I remember the experience vividly because it felt like I wasn't writing the poem.

My connection to Al continues. I collect his books, gathered with great effort at times. There was a bookseller who told me he had no Purdy books but after conversing on all things poetic, decided I was worthy enough, and went to the back, emerging with several Purdy gems, including my favourite, *Wild Grape Wine*.

There are a few things about Al I can't help but admire: his late blooming, which inspired me at forty-something to finally put a book of poems together, a.k.a. it's never too late to write a poem; his commitment to poetry— legendary, rare, and at times hard to understand given some of the sacrifices that were made; and the simple fact he wrote real poems that didn't look to be clever or academic or up or down. Just finely crafted here-I-am poems that relate on the level of the human condition. Our fake news world could use a lot more Al.

Laurence Hutchman, writer and professor, has published ten books of poems, co-edited *Coastlines: The Poetry of Atlantic Canada* and edited *In the Writers' Words*.

He received the Alden Nowlan Award for Excellence and was recently named poet laureate of Emery. He lives with his wife, the artist and poet Eva Kolacz, in Oakville.

My first encounter with Al Purdy's work was in grade thirteen when I read his *Cariboo Horses* at the Kipling Public Library. I was captivated by his poems about hopping freight trains across Canada during the Depression, working in the factory and the idiosyncratic character of hockey players. Here, I discovered a real voice of Canadian poetry and I learned that poems happen at the intersection of objective and personal history. Later he encouraged me in my writing and in a letter from Ameliasburg he invited me to be part of the anthology *Storm Warning 2*.

My PhD thesis was largely dedicated to his poetry… "Purdy captures a sense of the country and its people with clarity of expression that has rarely been achieved in Canadian literature. Purdy uses epigrammatic lines, appropriate allusions, original imagery, various rhythms and ritualistic diction."

My poem "Al Purdy's Place" is dedicated to him.

Ben Ladouceur completed a residency at the Al Purdy A-frame from September to November 2016, during which time he worked on his second collection of poems, *Mad Long Emotion* (Coach House Books, 2019). Ben is honoured to be a current member of the Al Purdy A-frame Selection Committee. He is also the prose editor for *Arc Poetry Magazine*, and his work has appeared in such publications as *Poetry*, *North American Review, Maisonneuve* and *The Best of the Best Canadian Poetry*.

Patrick Lane lives in the municipality of North Saanich on Vancouver Island with his wife, the poet Lorna Crozier, their two cats, Basho and Po Chu, and two large turtles, Drabble and Emily.

I was born eighty years ago and have written poetry for sixty of those years. In this I resemble Al Purdy. His early chapbook, *Poems for All the Annettes*, was an early major influence. I remember well reading it as I sat on rock by the North Thompson River near the sawmill village of Avola where I worked as a first-aid man. Purdy and I crossed tracks many times over the years, but our real friendship began in 1990 on Vancouver Island and continued until his death. One of the last favours I did for Al was to nail his deathbed back together after it collapsed under him. I remember Al standing shakily to the side holding on to his intravenous pole as he leaned against the wall, Eurithe encouraging me to hurry the job. He died a few weeks later, the bed intact. Over the many years of my writing life I have on the rare occasion wondered at my calling. At such times I have turned to the poetry of Al Purdy among only a few others to remind me why I was a poet.

Dennis Lee lives in Toronto. His most recent collections are *Heart Residence: Collected Poems 1967–2017* and *Melvis and Elvis*.

John B. Lee was appointed Poet Laureate of the city of Brantford in perpetuity in 2004 and Poet Laureate of Norfolk County for life in 2015. His work has appeared internationally in over five hundred publications and he is the recipient of over one hundred prestigious awards for his writing. The author of nearly eighty books, his most recent work includes (from Black Moss Press) *The Full Measure* (2015) and *The Widow's Land* (2017). He had several books forthcoming in 2018.

The statue that is installed at Queen's Park in Toronto was sculpted by my friends at the Negales Studio in the village of Highgate in southwestern Ontario near Chatham. (The studio is located in a converted hardware store once owned and operated by my great-grandfather Gustin Crosby. It is situated across the street from the elementary school I attended.) They were commissioned to create the statue by the Griffin folks in Toronto. I hosted several poetry readings there while they were doing studies for the statue. I called those readings "Reading to the Spirits" and dedicated them to the memory of Al Purdy. The readings were well attended—over one hundred people came. We read upstairs in the gallery with plaster busts of Purdy's head lying on the shelf near at hand like the busts of Roman emperors.

Jeanette Lynes is the author of seven books of poetry, most recently *Bedlam Cowslip; The John Clare Poems* (Wolsak and Wynn/Buckrider Books, 2015). Her second novel, *The Small Things That End The World*, was published by Coteau Books in 2018. Jeanette directs the MFA in Writing and teaches writing and Canadian literature at the University of Saskatchewan.

I remember the "Purdy revelation" moment vividly, despondent on my couch in my basement apartment in North York, struggling to feel connected to the Shakespeare text we were assigned by our professor. This must have been around 1980. Earlier that day, I had bought a book of poems by Al Purdy; I hadn't heard of him but a quick scan through the pages told me it was a far cry from Shakespeare—and it was. At last, a voice that spoke in my vernacular, that of rural Ontario. Only over time did I realize the erudition underpinning Purdy's work. But in that moment, I marvelled at the immediacy of the writing, the anecdote raised to art. I didn't know a poet could write about wrecked cars, beer, and construction workers. Discovering Purdy was a homecoming. My hands felt again the stones we cleared from our fields. The poems evoked how nature gets inside our houses, through cracks, no matter how hard we try to keep it out, and stake our authority in the world. Purdy's poems were quotidian, located, yet epic in scope. They felt authentic to me. They felt real. I've taught Purdy's poems many times over the years.

Kath MacLean's award-winning poetry, prose, non-fiction and films have been published and screened across Canada, the United States and Europe. Her most recent books are *Kat Among the Tigers* (2011) and *Translating Air* (2018). MacLean was the writer-in-residence at the Purdy A-frame for three months in 2015.

Susan McMaster's publications include poetry books and anthologies; recordings with Geode Music & Poetry and First Draft; and projects with artists, musicians, and writers such as *Waging Peace: Poetry & Political Action*, and *Branching Out*, Canada's first national feminist magazine. She's a past president of the League of Canadian Poets.

The phrase "death is yodelling quiet" from Purdy's "Wilderness Gothic," and the probably apocryphal story about the would-be poet who asked Al in a bar how he could write when it was so hard, have been touchstones for me, even while the drinking-man-among-men pose he cultivated was antithetical to my budding feminism in the seventies and my discovery of Canadian women writers. I never knew Al Purdy, know only the stories. But along with the roistering there are lovely words, and the quiet tale of a long and loving marriage. Thank you, Al.

Julie McNeill is a Toronto poet and graphic designer. She was an original member of George Miller's Bohemian Embassy, later Phoenix Poets' Workshop. She has given numerous readings across the country, as well as on radio and television. Her book, *Four Red Crescent Moons*, appeared in 1998.

Al Purdy has always been a presence in my world. A friend gave me the 1971 book *I am a sensation,* edited by Gerry Goldberg and George Wright and published by McClelland and Stewart, in which I first found his poems "Hockey Players" and "Complaint Lodged with LCBO by a Citizen in Upper Rumbelow." Then, while visiting a boyfriend's mother, I noticed an old poetry book that included poems by her but also the early work of Al Purdy. His work had evolved since 1944. You can't be writing and reading in Canada without having been touched by Purdy's easygoing "people's poetry."

I remember his readings: his booming voice, mirrored sunglasses and his rolled-up shirtsleeves. I especially recall an evening when a small group of us had gone along after a reading at U of T for a drink at the top of the Park Plaza Hotel. That was when you could still sit outside. It was a balmy evening and just being included made me feel like a "real" writer. I can still recall him sitting at the head of the table enjoying the attentive queries of a young woman who was writing an article about him. He'd made it, too.

Sid Marty, writer and musician, is the author of five books of poetry, five non-fiction books, two CDs of original songs and many magazine articles. His poems have been included in numerous school readers and anthologies. He lives with his wife, Myrna, at the foot of the Livingstone Range in southwest Alberta.

He was the kind of poet who could change lives, through the force of his poetry and the power of his friendship. Once he took an interest in you, he was a tireless champion—and critic—of your work and an indefatigable correspondent. But he hit the typer so hard sometimes that every period was a tiny bullet hole through the page. His letters were full of avuncular advice, such as, "Look, if you go teach you're crazy, not to mention lost!" (August 25, 1970), and racy anecdotes, such as, "I've burned half a dozen tiny almost unnoticeable holes in Everson's rug. Only thing to do to cover up is burn down the apt. bldg." (Feb 12, 1974).

I think that staying in touch with writers young and old as he aged kept him feeling connected and relevant, a sensation that inspired more writing to the very end. He seemed, for example, to have eyes on just about everything written back in the sixties and seventies. He "discovered" my own stuff in a little samizdat-style project of Andy Suknaski's called *Elfin Plot*. On the basis of that and some other obscure publications, he invited me to submit poems to the first *Storm Warning* anthology published by McClelland & Stewart, and later offered to write the preface for my first book of poems, *Headwaters* (M&S, 1973), an offer I gratefully declined.

But here is Al to sum up for himself in "Her Gates Both East and West," the last poem he ever wrote: "On a green island in Ontario / I learned about being human / built a house and found the woman / and we shall be there forever / building a house that is never finished."

Bruce Meyer is author or editor of more than sixty books of poetry, fiction, short fiction, non-fiction and literary journalism. His books include *1967: Centennial Year* (2017), *Portraits of Canadian Writers* (2016), the short story collection *A Feast of Brief Hopes* (2018) and the national bestseller *The Golden Thread* (2000). He was the winner of the Gwendolyn MacEwen Prize (2015, 2016), and was the inaugural Poet Laureate of the City of Barrie. He teaches at Georgian College and Victoria College at the University of Toronto.

Susan Musgrave lives on Haida Gwaii. She teaches in the University of BC's MFA program in creative writing. Her *A Taste of Haida Gwaii: Food Gathering at the Edge of the World* was published in 2015 by Whitecap. It won the Bill Duthie Booksellers' Choice Award, BC, and gold in the Taste Canada Awards.

I met Al Purdy in Mexico—in the Yucatan—in 1972. He and his wife, Eurithe, were travelling on poet's wages—staying in cheap motels, shopping for meat and potatoes in the markets, and cooking on their own hot plate. They must have blown up every electrical circuit in the Yucatan. I was all of twenty at the time; I'd never met anyone like Al, and though he was one of the most difficult men, in my young, nervous way, I grew to love him. (How could anyone resist a poet who takes his own hot plate to Mexico?)

Wherever I have travelled, Al Purdy has been there first. *And* written poems about it. No subject was too small or too awkward for Purdy, with his meat and potatoes small-town Canadian sensibility as big as the world's. His poems had a way of exuding what Seamus Heaney has called "some of the smelly majesty of living."

One day when I reach that "unknown country" myself, there is one thing I'll know: Al Purdy will have been there and written a poem about it, before moving on to wherever it is we go.

John Oughton was born in Guelph, but spent many summers in Prince Edward County. Recently retired as Professor of Learning and Teaching at Centennial College, he is the author of five poetry books, a mystery novel, and about five hundred reviews, articles and interviews. He is also a photographer and guitarist.

Al Purdy's poetry and life have influenced me in many ways. One is that he provided an exemplar of the non-academic poet, one who wrote from life and travel rather than theoretical or critical positions. He placed a key role in the development of a truly Canadian literature, with his many poems about ordinary jobs, different places across Canada, and his focus on the significance of place, and of local history. Also, his often long lines and works, and loose style, conveyed the sense that anything was possible in poetry, and one did not have to write sonnets or works following a given formal or thematic approach. Despite his persona as the shambling, uncouth small-town guy, he read widely, and used his knowledge of the classics and other poets to push poetry further towards honesty and validity, in the same way that his friend Milton Acorn did, becoming a genuine "people's poet." He and Robbie Burns would have shared some whiskey and a few laughs, had they been contemporaries.

Doug Paisley is a singer-songwriter from Toronto and a stay-at-home dad to his wonderful son Arlo. In his late teens he met Al Purdy several times at Purdy's poetry readings and was inspired by those encounters to pursue his own creative ambitions.

Autumn Richardson is a poet, editor and publisher. Her writing explores landscape, ecology, ritual and memory. Her poetry and translations have appeared in literary journals, pamphlets, anthologies and exhibitions in Canada, the UK, Ireland, Norway and the USA, including *Contemporary Verse 2, Room, Carte Blanche, The Goose* and *Five Dials*. She was awarded a Banff Wired Workshop Residency in 2015 and was poet-in-residence at the Al Purdy A-frame in 2017. She co-runs Corbel Stone Press, a small publishing house based in Canada and the UK.

Linda Rogers is a poet and fiction writer who has also written song lyrics, screenplays and social and literary criticism. She is a past president of the League of Canadian Poets and the Federation of BC Writers, past Victoria Poet Laureate and, like Al, a Canadian People's Poet. "Undeserving," he booms in heaven or hell, and she puts another big spoonful of ex-lax in his coffee.

> Al Purdy and I were in a relationship, yin and yang, bratty siblings, oyster and pearl. If irritation is influence, so be it. I never let Al have the last word if I could help it and I defended Eurithe to the death, not that she, lethal words being the arrows in her quiver, needed help either. Eurithe and I enjoy having lunch and talking about Al now that he doesn't eat with us any more and can't criticize our cooking. And we do sort of miss him. What I will say is that Al Purdy was a great poet, unique unto himself, a lover of music who found his own voice. That is what I learned from him. Tell it your own way. That is authentic. I hope that the many poems that were sent to Al as he lay dying find their way into this book. They gave him so much pleasure. But I will caution those who want to be him. Don't even try.

Rachel Rose is the Poet Laureate of Vancouver and the author of *The Dog Lover Unit: Lessons in Courage from the World's K9 Cops* (St. Martin's Press) and the editor of the anthology *Sustenance: Writers from BC and Beyond on the Subject of Food* (Anvil Press).

Her work has appeared in publications such as *The Globe and Mail*, *The American Poetry Review*, *Monte Cristo Magazine*, *The Vancouver Sun* and *The Press Democrat*.

F.R. Scott (1899–1985) was a trailblazer equally in law, literature and politics "in both official languages," as the *Oxford Companion to Canadian Literature* notes. Among his other contributions, he co-edited and contributed to *New Provinces* (1936), the first anthology of modernist Canadian poetry. His landscape poetry and social poetry strongly influenced many younger poets, including Purdy. Scott won the Governor General's Literary Award twice, once for poetry and once for non-fiction.

K.V. Skene's work has appeared in Canadian, UK, US, Irish, Indian, Australian and Austrian magazines. Her publications include *Love in the (Irrational) Imperfect* (Hidden Brook Press, 2006), *You Can Almost Hear Their Voices* (Indigo Dreams Publishing, 2010) and *Under Aristotle Bridge* (Finishing Line Press, 2015).

> Al Purdy's poetry makes me laugh, cry, sigh and feel totally exasperated. His poetry reflects Canada as it was, is and, likely, always will be.

Christine Smart is a poet with two books of poetry published by Hedgerow Press: *The White Crow* and *Decked and Dancing,* which won the Acorn-Plantos People's Poet Award in 2007. She is the artistic director for the Salt Spring Poetry Open Mic. She has lived and worked on Salt Spring Island since 1989.

> In the early eighties, I read Al Purdy's poetry when I returned home after five years in Scotland. He captured the Canadian landscape from coast to coast and lauded the vast diversity and complexity of this land. "Say the Names" is one of my favourites as well as "Arctic Rhododendrons."
>
> I met Al Purdy in person when he read at the Erotic poetry festival on Salt Spring Island in the nineties. A tall gangly man with a gruff voice, he wrote of love with depth and detail. He struck me as a "no bullshit" kind of writer. Afterwards, the poets gathered at Brian Brett's farm to discuss poetics and party. Al could seem a bit crusty but I saw through that exterior and enjoyed his warmth and magnanimity. He made me feel as though my words mattered.

Then one time, I had the honour of reading poetry as the opening act when he did a full reading at the Open Space Gallery in Victoria. I loved his voice and his confidence with language.

Karen Solie is the author of *Short Haul Engine, Modern and Normal, Pigeon* and *The Road In Is Not the Same Road Out*. A volume of selected poems, *The Living Option*, was published in the UK in 2013. A new collection, *The Caiplie Caves*, is due out in 2019. Born in Moose Jaw, she grew up in rural Saskatchewan, and now lives in Toronto.

Glen Sorestad's poetry has been published widely throughout North America and elsewhere. His poems have appeared in over sixty anthologies and have been translated into eight languages. His most recent books of poetry include *Hazards of Eden: Poems from the Southwest* (Lamar University Press, 2015) and *Water and Rock* (with Jim Harris; Lea County Museum Press, 2017).

Al Purdy's poetry has been an influence on my own poems ever since I first read his *Cariboo Horses* volume. Purdy's distinctive mix of narrative, conversational and lyrical within his poems was especially appealing to me, along with his humour and his sometimes acerbic or sardonic wit. His passion for Canada and his keen attention to historical detail also appealed to me and influenced my writing.

Lynn Tait is a Toronto-born award-winning poet/photographer, residing in Sarnia, Ontario. She has published poetry in more than ninety anthologies, including *Vallum, Contemporary Verse 2, Freefall* and the *Literary Review of Canada,* and in a chapbook entitled *Breaking Away*. Her photography and digital art have graced the covers of seven poetry books.

I lived in CFB Trenton from 1965 until the early seventies. A field, woods, and sand quarry behind my house were my playgrounds. Both Prince Edward and Hastings counties are well known for their land and rock formations, some quite rare. I have been a rock collector ever since. When I travelled back with my husband and young son, I was surprised by what had remained the same after more than twenty years, so the Purdy Festival was a great time to get reacquainted with the land in this century.

I started writing stories the year I arrived in Trenton, and poetry soon after. On a Saturday afternoon in Times Square, downtown Trenton's popular restaurant hangout for teens, Al Purdy was sitting in one of the booths. He did not look happy, or well, as he stared into his coffee. I decided to leave him alone.

Rob Taylor is the author of the poetry collections *"Oh Not So Great": Poems from the Depression Project* (Leaf Press, 2017), *The News* (Gaspereau Press, 2016) and *The Other Side of Ourselves* (Cormorant Books, 2011). *The News* was a finalist for the 2017 Dorothy Livesay Poetry Prize. In 2014 he was named one of the inaugural writers-in-residence at the Al Purdy A-frame, and in 2015 he received the City of Vancouver Mayor's Arts Award for the Literary Arts, as an emerging artist. He lives with his wife and son in Vancouver, where he helps coordinate Vancouver's Dead Poets Reading Series.

Al Purdy was the first contemporary Canadian poet I found on my own and read deeply, coming to his writing just after his death in 2000. His poems, and his personal history, made me believe it was possible that a Canadian kid with no immediately discernible talent could eventually make it if he worked hard enough. So I've worked, reading Al along the way, my writing going where it's needed to go, but also swinging back in its orbit toward Al from time to time (including, oddly, being called "the next Al Purdy" in the *National Post*). I've now lived in the A-frame and gotten to know Eurithe (as fine a person as they come! I'm sure Al didn't deserve her), and my general feeling of indebtedness to the man, his determination, his lopsided house and his poems has only grown. I memorized Al's poem "Untitled" many years ago, and still recite it when I need to remind myself that at the centre of my life, as it was with Al, "there is a loveliness / my heart knows."

Russell Thornton is the author of *The Hundred Lives*, shortlisted for the 2015 Griffin Poetry Prize; and *Birds, Metals, Stones & Rain*, shortlisted for the 2013 Governor General's Award for poetry, the 2014 Raymond Souster Award, and the 2014 Dorothy Livesay BC Book Prize. His newest collection is *The Broken Face* (Harbour, 2018).

Like the work of all real poets (real poets in my opinion anyway), Al Purdy's poems emit messages that find their ways into the brain folds of other people (and who can estimate how many other people?) and stay there and work their ongoing effects. Those "small purple surprises in the river's white racket"; that fox on the highway, with his "tail a flat red poker," his "feet red hammers hammering" and his "plans of the utmost importance"; that ice beginning to form, "tiny oblong crystals" that "seem to come from nowhere"; that momentary look in the eyes of his lifelong companion "an echo of the first tenderness"—to cite a few that often come into my own head—are examples from what is a long, long list of the conjurations he put together in his innumerable one- to two-page assemblages of words. Purdy's messages keep arriving, decades after the 1918–2000 individual is no longer around (well, no longer around in the ways we regularly acknowledge anyway); they keep sounding for me his visions of being human—and keep magically colouring the glass of Canadian poetry.

Peter Trower (1930–2017) was raised in BC coast mill towns, attended the Vancouver School of Art, and worked logging for twenty-two years. He published fourteen collections of poems and five books of prose. Al Purdy wrote the introduction to Trower's *Ragged Horizons* (McClelland & Stewart, 1978) and also to Trower's *The Slidingback Hills* (Oberon, 1986). In the latter, Purdy calls Trower the poet laureate of BC. "Trower unites nostalgia and the present tense in very nearly the same sentence," Purdy says. "A kind of nostalgia for now?" After listing several jobs Trower held over the years, Purdy says: "Trower's life was a lot like mine, with the difference that I was married and had a wife with notable gyroscopic abilities."

Grace Vermeer lives in Sarnia, Ontario. Her poems have won a number of awards, including the Lillian Kroll Prize in creative writing (Western University), the Monica Ladell Award (Scarborough Arts) and Honourable Mention in *Vallum*.

I was a newcomer to Al Purdy's poems. I admit I came with a chip on my shoulder, I'd met a few people close to Purdy who had stories—the walking wounded. However, when I started reading his work, I was quickly disarmed by his humanity, the images pulled me in. I couldn't refuse the human

I found inside the poems. He was doing what poets do, stalking his shadow, trying to understand his own life, the places, the people, the land.

If anything, the natural tone of his voice is teaching me to loosen up my writing, not edit so heavily, maybe don't kill off the roughness, maybe let some of the humanity just be. The last poems I wrote before I became very ill with Lyme disease were loose and long. It was a new style for me. When I came back to writing, my brain had changed, my poems got tighter and smaller. I like a well-crafted poem and there are several favourites I've found among Purdy's, but there is also something beautiful about his process of moving through a poem, following the images, letting it take you toward the epiphany, whatever wants to be found.

John Watson has won several major poetry prizes. He has published more than forty books in Australia. Many are chapbooks, small enough to hold in one hand without relinquishing the screen in the other—surely a recommendation. He represented Australia at the International Poetry Festival at Trois Rivières in Quebec in 2012. He lives in the Blue Mountains west of Sydney, but has travelled many times to Canada; indeed, one of his small books is titled *O Canada*. In Canada he has always noted the total disjunction between Australian and Canadian verse—in reception and availability.

Tom Wayman's recent books include collections of poetry, *Helpless Angels* (Thistledown, 2017); short fiction, *The Shadows We Mistake for Love* (Douglas & McIntyre, 2015); and essays, *If You're Not Free at Work, Where Are You Free: Literature and Social Change* (Guernica Editions, 2018). In 2015 Wayman was named a Vancouver Literary Landmark, with a plaque on Commercial Drive marking his contribution to the city's literary heritage. Since 1989 he has lived in southeastern BC's Selkirk Mountains, near Nelson. www.tomwayman.com.

Howard White is a writer, editor and publisher who published many of Al Purdy's books including his last one, *Beyond Remembering: The Collected Poems of Al Purdy*. He has written some thirteen books of his own including three collections of poetry, *The Men There Were Then* (Arsenal, 1983), *Ghost in the Gears* (Harbour, 1993) and *A*

Mysterious Humming Noise (Anvil, 2019). He lives in Pender Harbour, BC, where he co-founded Harbour Publishing and now serves as publisher of Douglas & McIntyre. He also serves on the board of the Al Purdy A-Frame Association, where he helped preserve the former Al and Eurithe Purdy home in Ameliasburgh and establish it as a residence for emerging writers.

Al Purdy was the first poet I ever encountered in the flesh and it completely changed my thinking. Up till that time I thought poetry was something handed down from on high and expressed in exalted language like Keats or at best, Dylan Thomas, but Purdy made me realize it could also be written about a junked '48 Pontiac by a slouchy, toothpick-chewing Ontario hoser. And still raise the hair on the back of your neck. This was at a noon-hour reading at UBC *c.* 1966. I met him a few years later at the Cecil Hotel in Vancouver in company with the poet Peter Trower and the painter/poet/ musician/boatbuilder Curt Lang. I drank more than I was used to, then Purdy generously invited us all to dinner where he was staying, which turned out to be the west-end apartment of the even more famous poet Earle Birney. Birney was away and Purdy began to have second thoughts about descending on Birney's crusty wife, Esther, with a bunch of hungry drunks, so we stopped on Robson and bought an armload of steaks, along with a bunch more beer. Esther took it better than we had any reason to expect and even assumed the cooking duties when it became clear Al was at risk of setting the building on fire. She obviously had acquired some experience at wrangling drunken poets over the years. I was tickled out of my skin to be in on such famous doings but tried not to show it, thinking this must be everyday stuff for the big-timers. I was amused to find Al later recounting the evening with great gusto and exaggeration, as if it had been memorable for him as well. We kept in touch after that and following one of his acrimonious blowups with McClelland & Stewart he asked if I would publish his autobiography, *Reaching for the Beaufort Sea.* We did that, followed by a collection of prose writings and his last three books of poetry. Coming to know the subtle mind and sensitive soul sheltered within the raucous Purdy exterior has been one of the great rewards of my years in the book trade.

Ian Williams is the author of *Personals*, a finalist for the Griffin Prize; *Not Anyone's Anything*, winner of the Danuta Gleed Award; and *You Know Who You Are*. His first novel, *Reproduction*, is forthcoming in 2019. www.ianwilliams.ca.

David Zieroth has published several books, most recently *the bridge from day to night* (Harbour, 2018). He lives in North Vancouver, BC

When I was first learning to write poems, I came across Al Purdy. What I heard in his poems was a voice that was sometimes public, sometimes private, sometimes both. Yes, the images and insights were there, but it was the particular voice that I connected with, one that was sometimes melancholic but also affable and wry. I was grateful to have heard him. And grateful again when he published my poems in his anthology *Storm Warning*.

ACKNOWLEDGEMENTS AND CREDITS

Thank you to all the extraordinary individuals who went out of their way to make this anthology happen. Thanks, of course, to the poets who submitted their work; to Eurithe Purdy, whose collection of tribute poems made a strong foundation for this project; to Tom Wayman, who took on the tough task of making the initial selection; to Kitty at Brick Books, who came to the rescue when Phil Hall's whereabouts prevented him from accessing his own poems; to Bruce Cockburn and his manager Bernie Finkelstein for permission to reprint "3 Al Purdys"; and to all the publishers who gave permission to reprint poems to which they hold rights.

Acorn, Milton. "Knowing I Live in a Dark Age" from *Jawbreakers*, Contact Press, 1963. "Poem for Al Purdy" from *The Uncollected Acorn: Poems 1950–1986*, Deneau, 1987. "Problem" from *The Brain's Target*, Ryerson Press, 1960.

Birney, Earle. "In Purdy's Ameliasburg" from *Selected Poems (1940–1966)*, McClelland & Stewart, 1966, and *One Muddy Hand: Selected Poems*, Harbour Publishing, 2006.

Bowering, George. "At the Cecil Hotel" from *The World, I Guess*, New Star Books, 2015. "The Country North of Summer" from *Some End*, New Star Books, 2018.

Braid, Kate. "Say the Names" from *Turning Left to the Ladies*, Palimpsest Press, 2009.

Cockburn, Bruce. "3 Al Purdys" from *Bone on Bone*, True North Records, 2017.

Currie, Robert. "Once in 1965" from *And Left a Place to Stand On: Poems and Essays on Al Purdy*, Hidden Brook Press, 2009, and *The Days Run Away*, Coteau Books, 2015.

Hall, Phil. "Essay on Legend" from *Essay on Legend*, Beautiful Outlaw Press, 2014, and *Conjugation*, Book*hug, 2016. "An Oak Hunch: Essay on Purdy" from *An Oak Hunch*, Brick Books, 2005.

Helwig, David. "Al on the Island" from *This Human Day*, Oberon Press, 2000. "Asleep at Queen's Park" from *Keeping Late Hours*, Oberon Press, 2015.

Hutchman, Laurence. "Al Purdy's Place" from *Personal Encounters*, Black Moss Press, 2014.

Lane, Patrick. "For Al Purdy" from *Last Water Song*, Harbour Publishing, 2007, and *The Collected Poems of Patrick Lane*, Harbour Publishing, 2011.

Lee, Dennis. "Tell the Ones You Love" from *Heart Residence: Collected Poems 1967–2017*, House of Anansi Press, 2017.

Lee, John B. "The Unveiling" from *Dressed in Dead Uncles*, Black Moss Press, 2010.

Meyer, Bruce. "Al Purdy: Voice" from *The Madness of the Planets*, Black Moss Press, 2015.

Musgrave, Susan. "Al Purdy Took a Bus to the Town Where Herodotus Was Born" and "Thirty-Two Uses for Al Purdy's Ashes" from *Origami Dove*, McClelland & Stewart, 2011.

Oughton, John. "Long Reach: Thanksgiving, 2000" from *Time Slip*, Guernica Editions, 2010.

Richardson, Autumn. "The Oracle," "Chrysalids" and "When the Deities Are Tended, Morning Comes" from *An Almost-Gone Radiance*, Corbel Stone Press, 2018.

Scott, F.R. "This Inn Is Free" from *The Al Purdy A-Frame Anthology*, Harbour Publishing, 2009, with the permission of William Toye, literary executor of the estate of F.R. Scott.

Sorestad, Glen. "Cactus Cathedral" from *And Left a Place to Stand On: Poems and Essays on Al Purdy*, Hidden Brook Press, 2009.

Tait, Lynn. "Challenging the Law of Superimposition" from *That Not Forgotten*, Hidden Brook Press, 2012.

Trower, Peter. "The Last Spar-Tree on Elphinstone Mountain" from *Between the Sky and the Splinters*, Harbour Publishing, 1974; *Bush Poems*, Harbour Publishing, 1978; and *Haunted Hills and Hanging Valleys: Selected Poems 1969–2004*, Harbour Publishing, 2004.

Wayman, Tom. "In Memory of A.W. Purdy" from *My Father's Cup*, Harbour Publishing, 2002. "Purdy's Crocuses" from *Free Time*, Macmillan of Canada, 1977.